Confessions
of a Billfisherman

JOHN ANGUS

Confessions
of a Billfisherman

The Halcyon Press

Published by
The Halcyon Press.
A division of
Halcyon Publishing Ltd.
PO Box 360, Auckland 1015, New Zealand.

Printed in China
by
Prolong Press Limited

No part of this publication may be reproduced, stored in a retrieval system or transmitted in any form or by any means, electronic, mechanical, photocopy, recording or otherwise without prior written permission of the publisher.

ISBN 1-877256-51-X
Copyright © John Angus 2005
First Published 2005
All Rights Reserved

Front Cover: "and capturing perfectly the beauty of my fish — a friend indeed."

Contents

A Friend Indeed 7
Reel Lucky 27
Third Time Lucky? 39
Three Broadbill And A Zoo Creature 53
If You Don't Weigh It, Don't Say It. 71
The Mission — Part 1 – "Paying My Dues" 87
The Mission — Part 2 – "Zoë, Zane And A Zebra" 97
The Mission — Part 3 – "Mission Accomplished" 111
Eldorado Revisited 139
The Nationals 149
Unfinished Business 169
The Unbreakable Record 195
Maps 212

A Friend Indeed

"Hello, this is Peter speaking."

"Hi, Peter! It's John calling from the UK, compliments of the season to you both. How are you doing?"

"Oh. John. Well. Not too good really. I suppose you wouldn't have heard. I'm sorry I didn't let you know but I have been a bit….., well, it's been a difficult year."

"Why what's up?"

"I lost my Jenny nearly a year ago."

"What?"

"Head-on car crash. I was the only survivor."

For a while I could not draw a breath. My blood ran cold, shivers ran up my spine and the hair on my head tingled as the shock of his words swept over me.

I had known Peter for about fifteen years and Jenny nearly as long, he and I were old fishing and shooting buddies. They had left the UK for New Zealand a couple of years previously and we had remained in touch intermittently, usually around Christmas time.

The previous Christmas I had even thought of paying them a visit with my family but his mother was coming so we had put it off.

Peter had made his money and retired in his thirties as a bit of a playboy, just before we had become friends. At the time I was still working hard to make my pile but we had common interests and he'd replied to an advertisement I had placed in the *Trout and Salmon* magazine for rods to join a small and exclusive syndicate I was putting together to fish the stretch of the Avon River that ran through my property and farm. We fished upstream dry fly for brown trout and grayling with great success *"and watched as the fish careered and leaped on the leader at the back of the boat, with the tag stick poised to strike."*

and over the years I developed one of the best fisheries of its type in the south of England. Together we also joined a new syndicate to fish for wild sea trout and Atlantic salmon at Peter Mantle's Delphi fishery in Connemara, western Ireland, where we dapped our live daddy long legs on the Loughs and fished our wet flies in the river. Jenny would often be with us. Together we had chartered boats to fish the wrecks in the English Channel for pollack, conger, tope and mackerel.

He bought a house in Hungerford on the river Kennet which also had good duck and pheasant shooting, so we fished for trout in the summer and shot over my land or his in the winter and we had a ball for many years until he had left for New Zealand with Jenny and his dogs where they became happy and settled.

I remained on the telephone with Peter for a couple of hours, mainly listening, as he revisited the awful tragedy for my benefit. At times he would drift off and lose the thread and it was plain that even a year later he was not well and had struggled alone to come to terms with the events that had left him a shattered man, deeply depressed.

"Would it be all right with you if I flew down for a visit Peter, perhaps we could go fishing?"

"John, would you? That would be just great, please come soon."

And so after the briefest of interludes, flights were booked, big game fishing gear packed and around the middle of January I left London for Auckland and then Whangarei where Peter would meet me and take me to his colonial-style house on a small farm north of Twin Bridges near the Bay of Islands.

I had recently sold the European computer leasing businesses I had managed for some years, made my investments and retired before I was fifty with the idea of catching as many marlin as I could before I got too old to wind the handle. With the world's biggest striped marlin also heading for the Bay of Islands I was hoping one or two would cross my path.

I left my wife and four children with a blank chequebook and a house in the middle of a major upgrade and took off to help my friend fourteen thousand miles away, the other side of the world.

As planned Peter met me at the airport at Whangarei and we went into town and had lunch in the Town Basin overlooking the marina and we talked. We talked for hours, then drove up to his house and talked some more. We talked for days. All the while he retained a haunted detachment devoid of the life and fire I remembered.

After the accident Peter had been in a coma for three days and awoke to find himself in a worse nightmare than any that could be dreamed. As the only survivor, four others had perished, the police had laid everything at his door and having no memory of the accident and without apparent witnesses, Peter was at the mercy of the system.

Now Peter of old would have fought ferociously to defend himself, he had studied law at University; his mother referred to him as "the Judge". He was a tough and intelligent negotiator, very argumentative and always right. But this was not the Peter of old. Dependant on anti-depressants, suffering from maybe some minor brain damage, he had given up easily, there was no fight left in him. He had accepted responsibility and was fined and after burying Jenny back in the UK with her family, had returned to NZ to become more or less a recluse, not knowing one day from the next, with no direction, no ambition, empty of all emotion and terribly lonely.

Over the days he told me more and more and things forgotten or down deep, rose to the surface and he gradually unburdened the load that had weighed so heavily and after a while we began to go out for drives and he showed me the sights. The Hokianga and Tane Mahuta, the giant kauri tree, Tutukaka, Pahia, Russell and Whangaroa where he had his forlorn Mariner 35 berthed at the splendid marina. We visited all the fishing clubs and saw the wonderful fish mounts, trophies, memorabilia and the recorded exploits of Zane Grey. We saw marlin being weighed in, striped marlin bigger than I had imagined, albeit long and lean January fish, just arrived and not yet fed-up and fat like they would be come April.

Peter's boat was not set up for game fishing, Peter, not being a good sailor, preferred snapper and yellowtail kingfish and fishing at anchor. So when the weather was good that was what we did. We caught snapper and trevally and kawahai and maomao but all the time my eyes were straying out towards the blue water.

After a couple of weeks Peter announced that he was feeling better and was going to try and come off his pills and if I wanted we could go out trolling for half a day to see how he went. Maybe sleep over on the boat, take it as it comes.

So we made preparations. I got the gear organised. Lures rigged, hooks sharpened, drags set. Although we had no outriggers strung I made up roller trollers and safety lines and we left the serenity of Whangaroa

Harbour and steamed out past Stevenson's Island, heading for deep water.

It wasn't a bad day, there was a long swell and a light chop and the wind varied between 10–15 knots, but it was a bit much for Peter and he suffered for my benefit as I urged him out beyond the 100 metre line. The sea remained green and cold.

There were a few other boats to be seen further out and a free jumping marlin hounded across the surface about half a mile away and we edged over to where it had been with Peter getting more anxious by the minute and me getting more excited and expectant.

We trolled up and down for a couple of hours before the wind picked up a bit more which was enough for Peter to want to head back, so we made for the shelter of the harbour entrance, dropped the pick and went back to the snapper fishing.

"Maybe you should charter a local boat John, I'm not sure I am ready for this just yet."

"That's OK, don't worry, let's fill the cooler with these bottom fish and relax and have some fun. I'll still catch more and bigger than you anyway."

"Oh yeah, you never did before. I caught bigger trout, a bigger salmon, in fact did you ever catch a Delphi salmon on a fly?"

"Shut up and pass me the pilchards, I see you've grabbed the best rod again and the best corner of the boat."

"Ho! Ho! I've got a snapper already! Get ready with the net."

"Get it yourself, I've got the hooks caught in my sleeve. Why the hell do you need two hooks anyway? That fish would fall through the mesh."

"Must be two kilos, look at it go!"

"Drop off you bugger, don't encourage him."

The fish went in the cooler and a fresh pilchard was lowered down. Peter was regaining some normality, I remember now what fishing with him was like, it was a contest with only one winner or he would be a bloody misery. I watched him as he concentrated on the freelined bait. On this occasion he could catch them all. His blood was flowing again.

Later, as we ran back into the marina to have dinner at the Gamefish Club, Peter said, "Look at those boats, they are the top performers at Whangaroa, they catch a lot of marlin and are inexpensive, only about $600 a day."

I looked at the pretty but old-fashioned displacement boats swinging on their moorings.

"You know Peter, you get what you pay for. I wouldn't by choice go out in an old boat like that, take you half a day to get there and back. There must be something sportier around, you know that money's not so important, I'm used to paying up to $1500 US in the Caribbean. You always were tight with your dough."

"Yes, and you always threw it around," he snapped back.

"You know what Peter, I think you are getting better." I said biting my tongue as my hackles bristled, "Let's go have a beer."

At the Club we got to hear the "stories". Stripies all over the place and a big blue marlin close to 600lb weighed in. We chatted to a few people and Peter told some how I was a keen marlin fisherman and desperate to set about the striped marlin. Someone said, "He should try *Primetime*, he ain't got nobody to go out with him," and they all laughed.

It was a joke but I didn't get it.

We didn't sleep on the boat and after a pleasant meal and a few sundowners on the deck as the sandflies devoured my ankles; we drove home in Peter's truck and for the first time had an early night.

"Let's take the XJS out for a spin, it's a lovely sunny day, I'll take the top down."

The next day Peter had a bit of sparkle and we pulled the Jaguar out of its garage and jumped the battery. We drove over to Opua and caught the ferry to Russell.

As we sat in the car on the boat, Peter said: "After you called me over Christmas and said you were coming I had to try and organise myself a bit and shake off the blinkers, anyway as a result I got involved with one of these internet dating agencies and just before you arrived I arranged to meet a girl who lives in Auckland and it went well."

"Well that's great Peter! Why didn't you tell me before?"

"Well, you were coming so I told her that as you were travelling such a long way and being an old friend, I would be giving you my attention for the month or so you would be here. It was really a hard thing for me what with Jenny not being gone very long but after talking with you on the phone I knew I had to try and get involved with things and anyway I like her, she listened to me and seems to understand my difficulty."

"That's OK Peter. I'd like to meet her, why don't you invite her up here."

"I was hoping you'd say that, maybe she'll come for the weekend, she's very tall and in her early thirties, divorced and very sporty like most Kiwis."

"Yes do that, maybe we can take her fishing, with the extra hand we could try trolling again if the weather's good."

Off the ferry we drove on to Russell where for the first time I saw a fully rigged game boat moored off the beach.

"Now that's more like it, look at that boat."

"That's Bill Hall's boat, *Te Ariki Nui*, he's the top guy, a legend, you won't get a charter on that one."

"So why's it on its mooring then if it's so great?"

"Maybe the weather?"

I looked out longingly across the bay, which was rippling and glistening in the warm breeze. "Oh, boy, this is murder." I thought to myself.

When we got back late that afternoon, Peter set to work on the nearly year's supply of post that was piled up in his office and we had a major clear out of papers and unopened magazines and general junk and I helped him sort out the fridge and freezers and kitchen cupboards where much of the stuff was months past its sell by dates or use by dates. These dates provoked an argument as Peter was reluctant to discard much of what I had collected claiming that the dates were manufacturing dates. Normally I wouldn't have cared less but thinking that this was too good a chance to miss I took the opportunity to press all his buttons and soon we were in the middle of a major row

"By the time I came up tight we were almost over the fish which had gone down to sulk and I began the hard work."

which I refuelled whenever it seemed like dying and he was soon going purple at the edges. In the end we both went off to bed not even agreeing to disagree and I knew another bend in the road had been navigated without any casualties.

"Pleased to meet you Cathy, have a gin and tonic after your long drive up?"

Peter's new friend had arrived on Friday evening.

They seemed very relaxed in each other's company and there was nothing to be gained by me sticking around so after a leisurely dinner, plenty of wine and a chat I made my excuses and left the couple to themselves.

The weather forecast was fantastic and we were all set to go to the boat in the morning and stay aboard for the weekend.

I was up early, had all the gear ready and was set for action.

Needless to say the other two appeared bleary eyed sometime before ten o'clock and it was apparent Peter was beginning to find some of his old self. Cathy like the famous beer had ways of "refreshing the parts other beers cannot reach." Ways not included in my repertoire, not for love nor money. Patience and a non-judgemental ear was the best I could provide and they're qualities not even my mother would normally attribute to me.

Wondering if I was actually going to see the ocean today, I was surprised when Peter suddenly and rousingly declared that we should hurry up and get going, clapping his hands enthusiastically whilst distributing the "Pahia Bombers."

Now, I don't get seasick but to "join the party", I did as bidden and was pleased to allow Peter to take charge, his confidence fast returning.

Our happy little band loaded aboard *Makaira*, we were about to cast off when a fellow called out as he walked along the dock.

"Hello Cathy, what are you doing here?"

It was a business acquaintance she had done work for in Auckland and he was going fishing too, on *Primetime*, with Roger, one of Peter's friends. They were planning to go miles offshore to some far distant seamounts and would be away for some days. I had noticed *Primetime* as we had arrived at Whangaroa, you could hardly miss it, and the big Salthouse stood out like a sore thumb amongst the tin boats and wooden hulls that lay silently against the floating docks.

We bid them well, threw them our warps and then none too expertly, edged our way out of the marina and past *Primetime*, a hive of activity as it shone in its slips. The fighting chair, bristling with heavy bent-butt rods and bright polished golden Shimano Tiagras, sat resolutely in the "cockpit from Hell."

"Bloody Hell, Peter, that looks the business, must be a private boat, eh?"

"No, it's a charter boat. Hasn't been here long and has really caused a stir up here; put the locals' noses out of joint I can tell you."

"Why's that?"

"This is parochial Northland, change is unwelcome up here. He's the new kid on the block, they'll give him a hard time unless and until he proves his worth and even then if he does he'll be resented, despised or hated even, you know what people are like."

"Sure do, you don't make too many friends on the way up the ladder, I certainly enjoyed treading on a few hands."

"John Angus, the master of understatement. One of your people told me once at one of your summer parties that you were known as 'the butcher' in your business."

"Surgeon maybe. I remember the guy; I closed down his branch operation in Manchester and sacked all his staff. My chairman wouldn't let me fire him because he fancied his wife but I got him eventually when he failed again in Greece."

"Yup, hard competitor."

"You can talk! But I'll catch more than you today."

"Oh yeah?"

"Yeah! You've got distractions."

Cathy blushed. I never did fight clean.

We left the harbour entrance and quietly ran towards the western exit with Stevenson's Island on our starboard side.

The three of us were sitting on the open fly bridge when *Primetime* blasted by us on the plane with a grim-faced man at the helm, a small thin cheroot jammed between his teeth.

Our vessel bucked around but Peter remained the right colour and I went down into the cockpit to prepare the gear.

With a plotter and sounder up top and also in the saloon I could monitor our progress and give Peter directions. I wanted to go out towards the 200 metre line and follow it as it arched back towards Cape Karikari and across Doubtless Bay. Marlin had been caught between

140 and 180 metres so rather than zigzag which would have been a bit technical for the driver, I planned running up the outer and coming back along the inner, thus avoiding many of the other boats which were much in evidence from the Ruahine reef and beyond.

It was a beautiful sunny day, flat oily calm with no wind to speak of. I could have been in the Bahamas. The current lines were easy to spot and clear blue water stretched everywhere.

Fishing in a straight line and being greedy I had every suitable rod I could muster set up and by the time we had crossed the 100 metre line I had two medium lures out, as long and as wide as I could get them on my Penn 50s and four other smaller tuna type lures and feathers on lighter outfits with either TLD multipliers or Baitrunners rigged with 20–30lb lines.

We didn't hook a marlin but we caught stacks of tuna. Mostly skipjack and a couple of small yellowfin. We broke off occasionally and the big fish got away. It was pandemonium but great fun. We saw whales and dolphins and a huge shark, maybe a white pointer, stuck its head out and looked at us and manta rays flew under the boat and shearwaters dived at the lures. It was one of those days when the ocean is alive with fish, it was wonderful.

With a bin full of tuna it was late in the afternoon when we dropped anchor inside "Stevies" and Peter and Cathy set about the small snapper as I kept them supplied with fresh tuna bait and mashed the berley.

Happy and tired we returned to the marina, got cleaned up and had dinner in the Gamefish Club.

"So what else do you know about this *Primetime*, then Peter?"

"Well I know he charges at least twice as much as anyone else."

"Yeah well, you get what you pay for, you know that. That's one hell of a boat. He probably burned as much fuel passing us as those wooden boats do in a day."

"Well you won't find me paying $2500 a day."

"It's still cheap by European or US standards."

"Yes but this is New Zealand. I don't think he's got too many customers. The One Base Tournament is coming up and I heard he's the only boat without a fare. It's a big laugh with the locals."

"Well it's certainly set up to catch fish, have they caught much?"

"I think so. On the board over there it says *Primetime* currently holds the striped marlin pin and has weighed a bunch of good yellowfin too."

"Well if I do decide to charter it'll be on that boat. Come with me, I'll pay. You haven't let me spend any money so far. You've paid for nearly everything."

"I'd go out for a day maybe but not for days like they do, I'd be as sick as a dog."

"You were fine today."

"Yes, when I'm at the helm or driving I'm normally fine."

"Well if we get a marlin tomorrow I won't need to charter and you'll be happy that I saved my money."

"I'll be happy if you get the beers in and pay for dinner."

As often happens with sea fishing the next day was totally different. The wind freshened overnight and the clouds were scudding across the blue sky but we persevered for most of the day without seeing a thing. How is it you can get two days like that? I know this is New Zealand but the ocean was barren and if we hadn't experienced the previous day, when everywhere we went there was bait sprinkling the surface, I wouldn't have believed it.

We had got under way full of expectation and I had left the small tuna

"the stretch of the Avon River that ran through my property and farm."

lures out of the water and concentrated on searching for "stick face."

I stayed in the cockpit the whole time and left the other two up top with Cathy taking the controls for luck but to no avail. I knew it was coming so I was not surprised when Peter said he was bored and cold and was heading back for a snapper fish. If I didn't know better I would say he was a Kiwi, they do love drowning pilchards. I guess it's still fishing and better than a kick in the balls but then anything is better than a kick in the balls.

It was nearly dark when we tied up and so decided to head home. Cathy would stay the night at the house and leave early in the morning and Peter and I would return to clean up the boat and maybe go out again, weather permitting.

Well the weather did not permit. A low had developed out of nowhere, a front was coming and Peter was pleased to have got two days on the water without losing a meal and had a freezer full of snapper bait.

Knowing we wouldn't be going out we made a leisurely start and didn't get back to Whangaroa until after lunch and was surprised to see *Primetime* back in and tied up.

Nick, a member of the *Primetime* crew stopped by as we were cleaning up, we'd met briefly in the Club a couple of times and he was always ready for a chat.

"So what happened to you then Nick, thought you were off for a few days?"

"Yeah well Peter, don't say anything but the charter found the going a bit rough; we never went even as far as the Garden Patch let alone the 60 mile ground and then this front popped up and they called it a day. How about you?"

"Loads of tuna but we never saw a marlin. So when are you off again."

"There's a lot of work on the boat just now and John wants to get it all done before the One Base."

"So he's got a charter then."

"Possibly, I don't know for sure, he's on the cellphone all the time trying to organise something. I know he's looking for another couple of guys to share."

"John here might be interested, sharing would make it cheaper."

"I don't do sharing, all or nothing. I've experienced sharing with strangers before, never again."

"What happened?"

"It was out of Montego Bay, Jamaica about 1970. It was $250 US dollars for the boat, I paid a quarter share. We hooked-up a huge blue marlin in the first fifteen minutes and a fat old Yank got in the chair and stayed there for nearly eight hours before the end of his big cigar touched the line and it was all over. The skipper went berserk and I vowed never to share again, unless with friends of course."

"Yes but this is a tournament, you can't just have one angler, we get doubles and trebles of stripies and especially yellowfin. Here comes John now, have a word with him."

A big man approached, loaded with gear and appeared preoccupied with his own thoughts. I was loathe to disturb him but said hello.

"Eh? Oh yeah, Hi. I thought this was a houseboat, didn't I pass it inside Stevies the other day?"

"I'm surprised you noticed."

"I notice everything."

"You didn't stay out long."

Suddenly I had his attention. Two can play this game.

"Bloody fair-weather fishermen. This is nothing; we could have stayed out, no trouble.

"Won't catch fish tied up. This'll blow out in a day or so. They decided to come back. They've paid for the whole trip anyway, so we are taking the time to make some changes on the boat and get set up properly for the One Base."

"I hear you are trying to put together a team."

"Trying. If you're interested, come and see me on the boat. I gotta go."

And he went. And so did Nick.

"Seems like a nice chap Peter." I said with hint of sarcasm.

"I reckon he's put himself under a lot of pressure, I'd be surprised if he makes a go of it up here. They say he used to be a commercial fisherman, trawlers."

"Poacher turned gamekeeper, you know all about that Peter."

"So are you going to go out with him?"

"Maybe."

"I think you should."

"Really?"

"Yeah, and if you do I can go down to Auckland and see Cathy."

"You randy old bastard, she's only just gone!"
"Don't be so rude. I have some shopping to do."
"Yeah, right."
"Did I tell you she made me have an aids test?"
"What?"
"I was clear."
"I don't doubt it."
"I made her have one too, you can't be too careful nowadays."
"I think I preferred you when you were quiet and depressed."
"Mmmm"
"What do you mean, mmmm?"
"I think maybe Cathy did too."

Ho! Ho! Ho! She found you out! Unleashed the tiger! Ha! Ha! So what's it going to be the old reprobate Peter or the new quiet and thoughtful Peter?"

"Not so much of the old."

"Well I am going to check out *Primetime*, the tournament is at the end of the week for five days and not long after that I'll be going home

---

"we fished for trout in the summer and shot over my land or his in the winter"

so if I am to catch a striped marlin I'd better do something because if the weather doesn't improve you and I won't get many more chances."

"Go on then. I'll clean off all this blood you spattered up the transom."

"That was your side of the boat!"

"It was your fish, it thrashed about everywhere, not under control."

"I'm going."

"Have fun."

"Have the last word."

"OK."

I wandered down the floating pontoon to the end slip.

"Permission to come aboard, captain?"

"Sure, come on up." Captain John Gregory called down from the big, glass-enclosed fly bridge; he was polishing what was already gleaming.

The rest of the crew were at work drilling holes in the covering boards to accommodate more rod holders.

There was no point in beating about the bush, they were busy so I got straight to the point, the five day Whangaroa One Base Tournament.

He had one guy definitely interested and some other possibles. I explained that at best I was prepared to fish with one other angler but other than that to count me out. It happened that the interested party was a novice angler looking for a marlin trophy and the others were a group of friends known to be keen to bring their own brewery with them and be generally uncontrollable.

"Well it's up to you. I want to go fishing not drinking, I'll go half share with the other guy at a reasonable price."

He got on the phone with the trophy hunter and came back with a figure that was acceptable to them and I was happy to match, so the deal was done. The two deckhands would also double as anglers if necessary; we had a team.

Peter dropped me at the Club the evening before the tournament for the registration ceremony and then was off to Auckland, post haste.

I put my gear in the grand forward stateroom onboard **Primetime** and returned to the Gamefish Club to await my fellow angler, Raymond, a second hand car dealer. If ever I had to describe a second hand car dealer, Raymond would be it.

On the first day the sea was a bit lumpy and the action was slow. We had our chances but the fish did not cooperate. Our car dealer spent most of the day being sick or feeling sick and carried on in the same vein on the second day when there was a good bite off the Cavallis and we managed to get pack attacked but miss out, much to the evident annoyance of the captain.

Lots of other boats reported hook-ups but lost fish and the stories were rife in the Club where seven striped marlin were recorded to add to the five of the first day. One boat had got two, we had blanked and the car dealer was being called a Jonah already.

On the third day the area outside the Cavallis was like Piccadilly Circus and it was hard to find room to fish. The skipper was getting visibly frustrated and that night in the Club, almost in desperation, made a change of plan that turned out to be a good call. The next day we were going to get out of there, we were to be away early and steam straight out to the Garden Patch; a long run but most other boats would not be able to follow and get much fishing time before having to head back for the weigh in deadline.

It was still very dark when we crept out of the marina and by the time the call came for "lines in", we were over the canyons watching dolphins and fast moving schools of yellowfin tuna working the bait.

I spent my "out of the fighting-chair" time searching the ocean for birds and leaping tuna, my angling partner retired to the day bed in the saloon, not interested in working for his fish.

I got the first fish, a yellowfin that dug in like they do and had to be battled onto the deck. I'd spotted a pod of dolphins that didn't look like dolphins and directed the skipper's attention. At the end of my stint I went up top and scanned the ocean waiting for them to pop up again and sure enough it was not long before my tuna was joined by another for our car dealer who had now got his sea legs, found his voice for the first time and was not slow in making up for three days of near silence.

Later on, with my hands wanting to encircle his neck, the worst thing possible happened.

Another fish engulfed the lure on the shotgun, the same that had accounted for the two tuna, only this time it was a striped marlin and at a quarter past the hour it was Raymond back in the chair.

I have to be honest and say I was sick. Not sick, berley sick, but sick, gutted sick.

I manned the camera dutifully and watched as the fish careered and leaped on the leader at the back of the boat, with the tag stick poised to strike.

With a dry mouth I joined half-heartedly with the celebrations and forced the issue regarding the tagging rather than taking of the fish. A subject the angler repeatedly complained about subsequently, having wanted to mount the head and bill on one side of the wall in his lounge and the tail on the other side of the wall in the kitchen.

A fate I could quite readily have recommended for him.

A lot more marlin were caught that day and one boat was now on three. With one day left and with only one marlin on the board the task was not yet hopeless and after all, I only wanted to catch one, one for myself.

We shot out again to the Garden Patch for the last flat calm day, hopes high, and it wasn't long before we spotted a pod of dolphins from which I managed to pull out another yellowfin tuna, but try as we might the marlin eluded us. We even stayed out after the "stop fishing" signal and missed weighing the tuna that had been cut up anyway.

As we headed in for the final prize giving, the skipper called me up to the bridge.

"I'm really sorry we couldn't find you a fish."

"Yeah, me too."

"Would you like to go out again tomorrow, my treat? We might do better with no Jonah."

"You bet, but it doesn't need to be free, you know."

"Let's see what happens, we'll get you a fish first."

I called Peter who had just returned from Auckland and was getting ready to come and collect me from the Club.

"Hey, Peter, no good, but John has invited me to go out again tomorrow, just for the day. Why don't you come too? You can man the camera, maybe even get a yellowfin."

"Yes all right, I'll bring my sleeping bag and stay overnight on my boat, see you later."

During the tournament a lot of big blue marlin had been reported, some totally spooling the reel in the first uncontrollable rush and all but one hooked and lost. One boat even lost a rod and reel; the rod holder and covering board being ripped out of the transom as the marlin hit the lure against a too tight drag setting.

Another boat, not in the tournament and fishing an area we had just left, had been surrounded by yellowfin trying to hide under the hull when a pack of big blues charged in, eating 40 kilo tuna like candy. They managed to catch a double of blues, quite a feat. All of which had served to increase my yearnings. The fish were out there and in quantity, they were hungry and as long as Peter wasn't a Jonah too it must be my turn.

Peter wandered up the dock from his boat and came aboard. He looked ten times the man who had met me nearly four weeks before. He was confident and glowing. It was a beautiful day already, the sun shone, there was no wind to speak of and as we left the harbour and eased into a long gentle swell inside of Stevenson's Island heading straight out to the seamount, Peter began throwing up over the side.

I felt terrible; he really became unwell very quickly. Should we turn back?

The crew were unsympathetic; after all it was flat calm.

Peter had taken his Paihia Bombers but on this occasion they didn't work.

After a couple of hours with no improvement I went upstairs to see the captain.

"It's up to you but this is your last chance to get a fish, we know they're here, you've worked too hard to give up now."

I went back down.

"I'm sorry Peter, shall we go back in. I hate seeing you like this."

"No, no I'll survive, I'm pretty used to it after all these years. I'll be OK if I lie down in here. Excuse me."

He ran out and just made it to the corner in time and folded over with only the tips of his toes touching the teak deck.

It was no good, I'd let him settle down and then tell the captain to head back.

Then all hell broke loose.

The prop wash and wake were alive with fins and bills scything through the spread of lures.

At least two reels went off, I eased the drag up on one fixed to a rod in the chair and it screamed and screamed as the line disappeared, too fast to witness. People were shouting. bodies were rushing about. We were still going ahead when a big blue marlin burst out at least 300 metres behind us and careered across the sea, going away really fast. Another gameboat that had been following, behind to our port, turned in, for all intents looking to cut us off. Only seconds had passed and the huge blue jumped off.

The other rods were still being cleared but the shotgun, which had popped previously was now taking off again and as I switched my attention to it a good striped marlin came out and hounded away, obviously well hooked and having a major panic.

With the captain shouting on the radio for the errant boat to clear out from behind us, I waited and waited as the line peeled off until it slowed and stopped and I began my retrieve with the big boat easing backwards and following the line that was zipping through the water.

Out the fish came again only to turn ninety degrees forcing the skipper to put the hammers down and we tore off in reverse as I wound as fast as I could. By the time I came up tight we were almost over the fish which had gone down to sulk and I began the hard work, slowly drawing it back up as it kited along beneath us.

Ten minutes of this and the fish came up about 70–80 metres away

"Peter Mantle's Delphi fishery in Connemara, western Ireland, where we dapped our live daddy long legs on the Loughs."

still lit up and swimming away. With most of the line back on the reel I could recover line more quickly and we went after the fish and the leader was grabbed.

"What do you want to do, it's a real good fish?"

"Let it go, let it go! But let me have a good look at it first."

"You sure? It's your first one and easily 125–135 kilos; bigger than any caught in the tournament, what a bugger, one day too late."

With the fish tagged I unbuckled and got out of the chair to inspect my prize.

It was magnificent.

The colours were extraordinary, lit up like a Christmas tree with fins erect and defiant I couldn't imagine how anyone could consider putting a gaff into it.

And there, right beside me, white as a ghost, matted hair plastered to his forehead, shaking and shivering, was Peter, camera in hand snapping away and capturing perfectly the beauty of my fish — a friend indeed.

I could have cried.

When Peter and Cathy saw me off from Whangarei airport a few days later I knew some important things had happened but needed time for it all to sink in.

Things that, before the year was out, would see my family immigrating to New Zealand.

Things that would see me back onboard *Primetime*, catching the big blue and winning the next Whangaroa One Base Tournament and collecting during the season all the wonderful trophies I had admired in the clubhouse and realising my dreams.

And Peter?

Well he was right about Cathy, she wasn't as impressed by the revitalised version, but a year or so later he bought a condo in Thailand, found a young Thai wife and now they flit from the farmstead in New Zealand to Thailand and back to the UK.

I don't see him much – I guess he doesn't need me anymore.

I'm always away fishing when he stops by but he knows where I am if he fancies a chat.

Just call *Primetime*.

Reel Lucky

Everyone remembers their first marlin, some might even remember all of them but the first is always going to be a special fish. Some poor folk go years and years without catching one and spend tens, even hundreds of thousands of dollars in the process. I'm glad to say that wasn't the case for me and although I had hooked a couple and lost them for one reason or another I didn't have to wait long and I can't say I had really tried particularly. It was always on holidays or odd times when business took me to some exotic location that I got the chance to fish blue water and then it seemed to be at the wrong time of the year when the marlin were not in town. Living in England didn't provide any opportunity at other times so all I could do was read about other's exploits, stare out of the window and dream about the time when I could quit working and spend time doing what I had longed for.

Ernest Hemingway, Zane Grey and the UK's Trevor Housby inspired in me the desire to go where they had fished, catch what they had caught and to experience all that they had seen as wonderful, exciting and awesome.

So when I got the chance I went to Florida, to Madeira, to the Azores, to the Bahamas and to the Caribbean. I caught lots of fish. I caught wahoo, I caught dolphin and tuna, I caught tarpon and snook, I caught bonefish and sharks and barracuda and mackerel.

I loved every minute of it but I never saw a billfish, ever.

There wasn't any to see. Wrong time, wrong place.

"Tough luck Brother, come back in July or September."

"Sorry Bud there's no marlin here in January."

"Hey, Easter is tarpon time!"

"I caught bonefish and sharks and barracuda and mackerel."

"Lo siento, pero, you're too late senor, here in October it's tuna and wahoo."

I'd like to say that it was all planned when it happened but it wasn't like that at all. In fact the first three marlin I caught were fluke out of season fish, nobody knew they were about, they shouldn't have been there. But, Hey, if you don't go fishing you don't catch fish, right?

It was coming up to Christmas.

I had flown my wife and four young children out to Florida for a four-week holiday.

I was in charge of the European businesses of a US company based in Boca Raton and they just happened to have a 78 foot Cheoy Lee motor cruiser and business had been good. They had extended the boat to include a platform at the stern complete with fighting chair and just for me; a brass plaque inscribed "Custom Built for John Angus".

I kid you not. It's true.

"Hey Johnnie, bring the family over, take the boat out to the Islands, relax, do some fishing, have a great time. You deserve it, buddy."

So I did.

I had been on *Quintessence* many times before and the skipper, John Manges, had become a good friend and when the six of us went aboard at Delray Beach on the Intracoastal there was only John and us for four weeks of blissful cruising the Bahamas.

The weather in Florida was unusually cold and at night it dropped into the forties Fahrenheit so after taking part in the famous Christmas "Boat Parade" we took a couple of days to quietly move down the Intracoastal to Fort Lauderdale and then Miami.

From there we crossed the Gulf Stream and first stop Bimini to clear customs, enjoy some cracked conch and have a couple of beers at Hemingway's old haunt, the Compleat Angler. After that we ran the Great Bahama Bank to the Berry Islands, planning to gradually move south and try to find some warm sun.

Taking this leisurely route meant slaloming around the big coral heads that scattered the sand like pieces on a chessboard but it also meant that I could have some sport with the big barracuda that hung on to the bibbed Rapala Magnums and danced across the surface, ploughing great bow-waves.

As you leave the Banks to approach the Berrys and Chub Cay you enter the Tongue of the Ocean and the Pocket, one of the most famous blue marlin spots in the Bahamas. A place where the bottom rises directly from "the deep" up to the Banks and a mere 20 feet. A crazy, swirling place where the upwellings create a wall of water and the bait swarms and congregates. A place where everything that swims can be found and the violence of life and death is played out like a maritime Serengeti.

It was here that we decided to really begin fishing and to zigzag our way along and across the edges of the drop off towards Chub Cay, the most southerly of the Berry Islands and one that was still recovering from Hurricane Andrew.

At this point I should remind you that the "crew" comprised the skipper who was high above, yards away and can't see the fishing platform, and me. So I had to do everything but drive the boat. The tackle was made up from whatever I could find on the boat plus some items I had brought with me from the UK and those I had purchased in Miami on the way.

The rods on the boat were 30lb class "Tuna Sticks" complete with reels of a make I dare not mention. John's 20lb outfits with "Baitrunner" reels and my own UK-built 50lb class boat rods designed for wrecking in the English Channel, longer and softer than those used for trolling, with matching reels loaded with 40lb line.

With what I could scramble together I had rigged two ballyhoo deadbaits covered with orange and yellow skirts, a couple of tuna feathers on the light gear, a wahoo lure on a planer, all on wire leaders and a medium purple and black softhead — just in case.

With the skirts over the ballyhoo baits we could tow them a bit faster than normal and I was fairly happy with my mixed spread that was designed to cover all the bases.

I caught wahoo and barracuda when we got too close in and the palaver when we hooked-up was pathetic but we always managed and we had great fun, especially with multi-strikes on dolphin, when sometimes I'd be trying to play three at once and getting in a fine mess.

Because the captain and I couldn't see each other, unless we had a volunteer to act as relay, John would have to run back from the controls and peer over from the high bridge to see what was going on. It was crazy but we didn't care, we were filling the refrigerator with some of the best eating fish in the sea.

Well it was an overcast sort of day, warm and humid. The ocean was pretty flat and with no more than a gentle breeze to affect the long swell, it was comfortable and pleasant.

Not having outriggers or even stingers, everything was run from the rod tops with no drop backs. It was less hassle for me on my own and as the hooks were often picking up weed I was pretty busy and as it was I didn't see the blue marlin eat the ballyhoo but when the reel screamed, I screamed, grabbed the offending rod and pushed the drag up a bit. The boat was still going ahead and with a full squad on relay I walked around the platform and wound back as many of the other baits and lures as I could, leaving the rods in their various holders. I didn't know what sort of fish I'd hooked but when a marlin of about 300lb burst out and began careering fast towards our starboard, there was a cry of "Marlin!" from up above.

A large belly was forming in the line but the weight was coming on and I could feel the pressure increasing as the fish continued its aerial manoeuvres until unexpectedly the line broke.

Actually it wasn't the line, it was the swivel.

When I examined what I got back I found that the swivel was corroded in the barrel.

"Hey, man, that was a blue marlin. What happened?" the skipper shouted down.

"Tell me about it. We need to get some new equipment. We can't fish with some of this junk." I was disappointed and ready to blame anything but really the fault was mine. I should have checked the gear more carefully.

Nevertheless we'd had a shot from a marlin and hooked him good and everyone was as excited as if we had caught it.

Even after all these years I still have a picture in my mind of that fish jumping away to freedom.

We were still some days away from Nassau and tackle shops so fishing was put on the back burner and we visited a pal of the skipper who owned a property on Frazier's Cay next to Chub Cay.

Vince had a lovely place and a posh new dock for us to tie up to. It was Christmas Eve and we were invited to stay. We spent Christmas Day playing the new board game Fishing Frenzy, cracked a piñata on the beach and had a wild barbeque that included lots of fresh fish.

It was fun, gentle and pleasant fun.

Poor Vince. He disappeared a few months later and was never found.

Drug running was still a big deal in the Bahamas and it seems as though Vince became shark food for some reason or another, God bless him.

After leaving Vince we ran the 35 odd miles to Nassau, or Paradise Island and Hurricane Hole Marina to be exact. On the way we were confronted by nasty electrical storms which we had to steer around using the radar but still nearly bumped into a couple of gigantic, spectacular and intimidating waterspouts. (Tornado of the sea.)

Paradise Island is great fun with Sol Kirzner's fantastic "Atlantis" complex and the world's best aquarium. We had a ball but kept out of the casino.

The tackle shop nearby had all we needed and it was with more confidence that we set off a few days later for the Exumas and Highbourne Cay for the New Year.

Nassau is a bit of a shock to the system after the solitude of cruising the Banks and ocean between the island groups and the peace and beauty of the Exumas was next for us and we couldn't wait to get back there for lobster and conch pistol salad.

The New Year's Eve party at Highbourne is the highlight of a lot of folk's calendars and the millions of dollars of big boats there was testament to the popularity of this great family event and they were packed in like sardines.

We crept away the next day leaving them to recover and for us to continue our adventure.

I soon had the gear in the water.

We had to run a bit wide to keep outside the protected Exuma Cays Land and Sea Park; which at 176 square miles and created in the 1950s was the world's first and therefore oldest maritime park. We were going into Waderick Wells Cay that night where the headquarters are situated and moor up in one of the Bahamas, most pristine and beautiful natural harbours.

The first bite came on the planer and I reeled a small wahoo to the boat for our dinner.

By running fewer rods I could relax a bit more.

It was just as well.

We were off Norman's Cay and the family were all shut up inside the air-conditioned saloon watching the movie "Little Giants".

I was lounging in my fighting chair watching the lures and the skipper was up top, probably looking at charts.

Bob Marley was wailing through the speakers, "I don't wanna wait in vain", when the ballyhoo with the yellow skirt in the long left position got *"a platform at the stern complete with fighting chair and just for me; a brass plaque inscribed "Custom Built for John Angus."*

whacked and the reel zipped for a second or two, and then stopped.

As I grabbed the rod and stood up I saw a marlin bill spear out of the water, collect the bait, turn and tear off. With the drag set lightly it was lucky I didn't get an over-run before I pushed up to strike and the fish burst out, leaping and thrashing in abject panic.

It wasn't a big fish but felt perfect on the 30lb outfit it was attached to.

The boat was still going ahead at trolling speed and the line was rapidly disappearing from the reel.

"John! John! Hey, John! Stop the boat!"

By now the fish had gone down and there was nothing to see on the surface.

"What's going on, Man?" A black-bearded head appeared.

"I've got a bloody marlin on here, do something. Quick!"

The head disappeared the boat slowed and then began to reverse. The ocean poured over the platform threatening to wash me away, so I retreated back up the stairs, winding like crazy.

"Hey! Stop! I haven't got the other gear in!" It was already too late, one line was being collected, so I paddled back down and set its drag to sunset. The rod heeled over and the line snapped with a crack.

"Aw! Shoot" The black-bearded head appeared again. "I'm coming down, hang on Buddy!"

As the boat stopped other bodies were appearing topside, between us the gear was cleared, camera was employed and the fight was on.

Then the reel handle came off.

"What the? Hell's teeth! I've got a problem!"

The wooden handle had come off of the spindle of the reel whose name I dare not mention.

Wearing a glove and pushing the handle back on the spindle and remembering to hold it on, I got winding and working again.

In the skirmish the fish had taken the chance to get as far away and as deep as it could.

With my relay in position and reporting well to both parties I hauled on the line and was recovering great sweeps, with the reel handle coming adrift disconcertingly, until the fish was just circling beneath us, taking a breather and not wanting to come up any more.

Now was when I could have done with the 50lb gear.

We got the boat downwind of the fish and by letting out some line as the windage collected the big boat, and then holding as hard as I dare, the fish planed up and we got it close on the leader.

John came running down from above and the fish made a final effort, throwing water everywhere and somehow amongst the spray and flailing fins John grabbed the bill and held on tight. With no transom for protection it was like a rodeo with the fish bucking John around the platform until it stunned itself by crashing into the boat.

"Quick, get the hook out and let's get this sucker out of here," urged John, not wanting any more excitement.

"You hold onto the bill, right, hold tight."

"Just get on with it, I've got it. Don't worry."

I nervously knelt down and wriggled the hook free with a trembling hand from the corner of the marlin's mouth.

The fish was upside down, looking worse for wear and displaying little colour. With the hook out John pulled the fish upright and held it in the stream to recover. Before long the fish switched its lights back on and seemed keen to be on its way. As it glided back down and out of sight John stood up and grabbed me in the most fearsome bear hug, forcing the air out of my lungs and making my ribs crack.

"Man, we did it, we got a marlin! Man o' Man, a marlin!"

John had never caught a marlin before, even after countless years fishing with his dad and his grandad and they'd never caught one either.

My, we were happy when we arrived at Waderick Wells and took the dinghy over to the house where they were having a bit of a do.

John had popped over the side, cut away the line from a rudder and prop, and miraculously recovered the lure and leader.

I stood amongst a throng of people and supped from my glass of white wine. A man in a khaki-coloured shirt with an official looking badge embroidered on its breast pocket, sidled over to me and spoke.

"Caught a marlin, eh? My, that's some feat. This time of the year there's not usually any about," said the park warden. "Was it a white?"

"Uh, I dunno, I assumed it was a small blue," I replied, surprised and wondering how he knew about our fish.

"Looked like a white."

"Eh?" I was even more surprised.

"Yeah, I was watching you through binoculars from my patrol boat, you were only just outside the park. Probably were at times. Here, take a look in this book, see what you think." He handed me a glossy tome describing the fish found in and around the sea park.

Well, sure enough, judging by its tall dorsal, it was a white marlin and a big one at that, around 120–130lb was the guess.

So my first marlin was a nice white, almost poached and not very professionally attained but very satisfying nevertheless and a small precursor to what has followed.

We left Waderick Wells the next morning but didn't get much chance to fish again after that, I'd used up all the ballyhoo and we stayed on the shallow Banks side of the Exumas on our continuing run down and anyway, just as we were about to leave Staniel Cay and Thunderball Cave to go on down to George Town I got hailed on the cellphone.

"Hey Johnnie, we need you in Dallas on Monday, you gotta come back." It was Phil, my boss. "Where are you, Staniel, right? We'll send

"I nervously knelt down and wriggled the hook free with a trembling hand from the corner of the marlin's mouth."

the Sabreliner to pick you up at the strip there. Have a nice day. Bye."

"Hey, Phil! Don't go. We got a marlin!"

"You did what? No kidding? Hey Sonny, come here, you gotta hear this! Johnnie got a marlin! Son of a gun!"

"Yeah, and the reel fell to bits."

The reel whose name I dare not mention, although I will say it wasn't a Penn, nor was it a Shimano. Needless to say I have never used one since, I am too superstitious to even contemplate the prospect.

So superstitious, that the shirt I was wearing has become my revered, all time lucky marlin fishing shirt, never worn at any other time and kept safe with the lucky hat, and the lucky fishing shoes and shorts, and the lucky belt, and the lucky sunglasses.

Oh Yeah! Of course, and the lucky Bob Marley CD.

"The fish was upside down, looking worse for wear and displaying little colour."

Third Time Lucky?

It's funny how things turn out sometimes, fate intervenes and what at first seems disappointing is in fact, a blessing in disguise and it all works out well in the end.

We had intended to fish the Whangaroa Junior's Tournament and I had chartered *Primetime* and paid the entry fees for my three fishing kids, Gemma (16), James (11) and Robbie (7).

The four of us were onboard and getting in some practise when alas, the message came through that the weather had caused the postponement of the tournament for a week. We couldn't fish the following weekend and the boat was booked anyway by another party and no suitable replacement was available to us.

As we were relatively unaffected by the weather on a big boat, we carried on fishing regardless. The rules of the tournament would have restricted our fishing area anyway and as nothing of any note had been hooked north of Cape Brett as yet, we turned our attentions to where the action was really happening – outside of the Poor Knights Islands.

Reports of big blue marlin hooked and lost, had reached the ears of Captain John and Pete Saul the Tutukaka guru had suggested that *Primetime* come down and steal a couple from under the noses of the locals. So we crept down to surprise them!

We fished our way down on the Friday and had watched the boats near Cape Brett trying to catch yellowfin inside us where the birds were working over the cold green water. We had dropped Robbie off at the fuel dock at Opua on the way as I had let him down by forgetting to give him a pill and he was feeling poorly. After that it was overnight at Whangamumu and out early before anyone else had left Tutukaka. A few

"James was summoned and within minutes he was under green water winding like crazy as we hunted down his fish"

"wind, wind, wind!" came the shout from above.

circuits around the newly installed FAD outside the Poor Knights Islands found nothing at home so we headed straight out into the blue water.

Neither Gemma nor James had fought a marlin before and the plan was for marlin strikes to be handled by Dad — well, we were not in the tournament any more — and for them to deal with tuna or even spearfish.

Well, sure enough, a strike occurred and I duly went to the chair and soon eased a small striped marlin into the waiting hands of the mate. Tag in, few photos, release and the first fish of the season was quickly reported to Whangaroa Radio. Congratulations all round and we were off again.

"Now listen Dad, this isn't fair, we're getting bored, we were supposed to be fishing this weekend, you can't have all the fun, and you have to stand aside now." Gemma was adamant.

"But you heard what Captain John said, you're not ready for marlin yet, you have to cut your teeth, learn the ropes, earn the right, you have to..."

"No way Daddio, we won't let you get to the rod, you probably told him to say all that anyway. James, don't let him get onto the deck."

At that, the rigger popped, the reel began screaming and James shot past me and whilst Gemma stood in my way, he pushed up the drag.

"Did anyone see the take?" shouted the skipper from on high, "Did anyone see the fish?"

As if in reply the sea erupted and a big blue marlin, just about as demented as it could be, began the usual theatre 200 metres behind us, before heading for Fiji.

"Quick now James, lift out the rod, get in the chair," urged the mate as the colour drained from James' cheeks.

"Dad! You do it, it's too big, look at it go! I can't do this."

"Come on James it's your fish," urged the mate again, "Come on now pick up the rod, quickly!"

So the little chap did as instructed and clipped himself to the rod and gripped the seat with both hands as the line ripped off the reel and the fish performed for us in the distance. The realisation of what he had done was now falling over James like a thunder cloud, sending him past red straight to brown alert but gradually as he saw that he hadn't been dragged into the ocean and trolled like a lure, he began to relax a little and focus on the task.

"You're stuck to it now James," said the mate at his side. "You have to play it yourself. It's got a lot of line out now, ease the drag back a bit, that's it. You'll be fine. Ready when you are John! OK James, get ready to wind the handle as fast as you can. As soon as you feel the pressure come off the rod, get cranking! We are going after it now, get ready!"

The boat slowed and stopped and off we went, ten knots backwards causing James to disappear under a wash of green water that sluiced over the transom. As the boat broached a swell, James reappeared, dripping and still winding hard, as if nothing had occurred. The water was sloshing up my calves as I steered the fighting chair and things were floating in the cockpit.

Ten minutes later and we were on top of the fish.

Johnno, the other deckhand, opened the stern door and the sea drained away from around our feet.

The fish was going down.

"You'll get a rest now, James," I said.

"No he won't, not yet. Push the drag up a bit James, not too much," called down the Captain.

"HELP!" James yelled as his bum came off the chair and he clung onto whatever he could as he was pulled upright.

The marlin, possibly feeling a bit more pressure, changed tactics and came up fast clearing the water behind us.

"Wind. Wind. Wind. Wind!" came the shout from above.

James got back to collecting the line and as the boat hurtled back towards the fish the leader was there and we were so close, oh, so close, just a tantalisingly few metres out of reach but the fish, no doubt sensing the urgency of its situation, went down.

Down and down and down...

"I can't do it, it's too strong, and it's too big. Dad! You take it. Oh why couldn't I have got the stripey and you had this one? Oh! It's pulling me in!"

After a while the loss of line slowed and the fish began to sulk. The crew were up top with the skipper and they were deep in conspiratorial whispering, heads together, at first shaking and then nodding in agreement.

They returned.

"OK James, you have to do some work now. You're going to lose some line but then you should get a lot more back."

As the mate resumed his place at the boy's shoulder the skipper started the fast circles to starboard to lead the fish and get it swimming up and on the move. Once he got the hang of it, James was soon working like an old hand, pumping and winding, using the swell to get more line on the drop and making more line each spin than he was losing. The fish was coming up and James was winning and looking determined.

This routine is hard on a prop forward let alone an 11-year-old and he was getting tired and hot and as is often the case with youngsters any small setback damaged his confidence. We provided all the encouragement we could and he was doing great until the great fish decided enough was enough and went down again and kept going right to the bottom.

"At last! James got his fish, the tag was in and pictures were taken and the celebrations were loud and long!"

James was heart-broken, he had taken all the fish could come up with for two hours but this was just too much for him, all that work to get so close, then more line than ever had disappeared from the reel. For the next half an hour James put all he had left into trying to get the fish up but he got nowhere and the realisation that all was not well crept ever more into my head.

The fish had sounded and died.

"You have to try James, or it will all have been for nothing." I strapped his knees with crepe bandages to provide some support and Gemma held his feet down on the footrest.

The little chap pumped and wound as the agonising task of planing the fish up commenced.

"Feeling a bit put out we sulked off and went fishing for yellowtail kingfish instead."

He made some progress but whenever a rest was required the fish started to sink again head first making the weight unbearable again. After three hours and having given his all, James went limp in the chair and I called timeout.

With the fish to be disqualified it didn't matter anymore so we unclipped him, lifted him out of the chair and I took his place in the hot seat.

As I took the weight myself for the first time I was lifted straight up out of the chair and straining hard to hold on I could not believe that he had managed as he had done for so long.

Putting my weight on my heels and rolling back my right shoulder I got to work.

Once I got the head of the fish up and coming, the rest was pretty straightforward and after thirty minutes the fish burst through the surface like a missile and settled back with a surge of water.

Minutes later it was on the deck — stone dead.

A great party was had at Tutukaka that night where we were received with tremendous heart and great kindness. James was treated to a deserved heroes welcome, stood proudly by his 240 kilos of blue marlin and was thoroughly overwhelmed.

The next day an even bigger blue marlin rushed off with a lure and in the proceeding scramble for the rod and delay whilst fighting over whether it was to be me or Gemma, I screwed up and the fish was gone.

Gemma spent the next two days sulking in the corner of the cockpit and I became persona non grata with all onboard.

As a result of all this I had to agree to sponsor another trip for Gemma and James when Gemma returned at Easter from schooling in the UK.

As luck would have it *Primetime* was booked but the captain recommended Chris Ash on *Independence*, so when April came around it was aboard the 45foot *Bertram* that the three of us set off once again. This time for the Three Kings!

I don't suppose many kids get to go to the Three Kings and the stories of bad weather and even worse sea conditions had made my two a bit nervous but I had just got back from a successful first trip there myself aboard *Primetime* when I caught two broadbill, four marlin and some 30kg kingies, so expectations were running high for a good trip.

Primetime was going back up again too so some competitive "needle" was expected and looked forward to. Especially as we had played a "nice" trick the week before by washing out all the broadbill blood as we ran back past *Independence* to recommence our drift. Thus shaking off any unwanted sharks and leading them nicely to the tuna baits drifting behind Crash's boat.

As this was the kids' trip I was relegated to deckie 3rd class behind the two crewmembers. Gemma was first up and sure enough, half way from North Cape, in the middle of nowhere, a nice fat striped marlin hung on and Gemma duly tagged her first marlin.

James of course, was now next and within a few hours we had the live baits out on the Middlesex Bank and James was ready in the chair. But when his bait was taken then so did another. I went to the other rod in the holder on the port side and James' fish came out of the water firmly hooked but — Oh! No! — It was wrapped up in my leader! Not again!

James was playing a fish certain to be disqualified unless it got free from my line quickly.

No such luck and as James fought his fish for twenty minutes I reeled in the slack line on my rod to keep it out of harms way. The tag went in and James was ecstatic and none of us had the courage to tell him that it wouldn't count, so we agreed not to, hoping to get him another. The problem was that I couldn't put him back in the chair immediately or the game would be up, so we kept the same rota.

Later I was in the chair on a fish but I managed to lose it, much to the captain's dismay.

Next day *Primetime* arrived to catch bait just as we were leaving the Kings for the Middlesex Bank and we were out fishing first.

"Oh boy, this is great!" Maybe we could find a couple before they joined us.

As time went by we were joined by *Bwana*, (with what looked like a bunch of sumo wrestlers onboard), *Ultimate Lady* and then *Primetime* who immediately got a quadruple strike and then got bites all morning.

Feeling a bit put out we sulked off and went fishing for yellowtail kingfish instead.

As it was pretty rough it was agreed to only fish one rod at a time and for the kids to use the chair. James went first and as we drifted over 100 metres of water with the live koheru down 40 metres of it, Bang!

With James handling the 24kg outfit a bit easier than the 37kg he got to work on a torpedo and twenty minutes later after a wonderful scrap a *"twenty minutes later after a wonderful scrap a fish bigger than James was on the deck."*

"Gemma… had caught a new National and World Female Junior Record kingfish at 28kg."

fish bigger than James was on the deck. It looked like 40kg and a record for sure.

Meanwhile, as we were mulling it over Gemma had quietly been lowering her live bait and, Bang!

Here we go again.

Another twenty minutes and the same result, only a bit smaller.

Wow! It looked like it could also be a record!

With both fish in the cooler with some ice that had been floated over in a chilly bin from *Bwana*, we eventually followed *Primetime* to the broadbill grounds and the kids took the opportunity to get a well-earned sleep.

Towards the end of the night as the captain slept, I tagged a mako to add to a whopper I'd got two days before and we crept past the other boats and back towards the head of the drift.

But we kept going, quietly creeping away so we could be first back on the Middlesex Bank marlin grounds.

Just on daylight I hooked-up onto a nice striped marlin that wanted to take us back to the broadie grounds. As we hurtled backwards in hot pursuit, *Primetime* appeared on the horizon and we all three of us, boats and fish, converged towards the same spot. Just at the right moment the marlin leapt out in front of *Primetime* and as they took avoiding action, we took the opportunity to get on top of the fish and get the tag in just as we passed. In jubilation I raised my arms aloft and felt honour was restored.

By now the kids were up and spewing that I had stolen a couple whilst they were piling on the zeds. (tee, hee). So yet again I was banned from the cockpit and sent upstairs to watch from a distance.

As often happens at the Kings the weather began to deteriorate and word came on the radio that we should be getting out of there soon, so it was with great reluctance that we headed off but via the King Bank where *Harlequin* was having some fun. The skipper was asleep again as we bashed our way across a maelstrom current line and gloom was everywhere as we approached the King Bank with the sea rising and the swells getting bigger and bigger.

I called Gemma aside and explained about the situation with James and she agreed to let him have the next marlin strike should we get lucky before it all went tits up.

At 2pm two live baits were out and one got bit immediately.

James was summoned and within minutes he was under green water winding like crazy as we hunted down his fish, which was hounding across the ocean only 30–40 metres away. Up and down the swells we went keeping pace with the fish, which made the mistake of turning and we were on it like a cat.

At last! James got his fish, the tag was in and pictures were taken and the celebrations were loud and long! It was the smallest of the trip but it was legal and I was delighted.

As it was, there was still time for another fish and what a fish it turned out to be.

With me still banned, it befell Gemma to play the next marlin, which hooked-up an hour later and this one like the last, took off on the surface, down swell and right behind us – but this was bigger and faster.

At first it was one swell away.

As we were on top of a swell the fish was leaping off the top of the next. The skipper was having to hold the boat back to stop us zooming down into the back of the following four-metre swell as the fish disappeared and, as we powered up the back of the next swell, the fish was nearly two swells away.

The sea was all over the cockpit and the tuna tubes had been blasted out and were crashing around my feet. Up we came to the top of a swell with Gemma cranking hard. The fish leapt off the top of the swell and just as it got airborne, the line came up tight and pulled it off balance making it turn in the air.

"Wind, Gemma! Wind! Wind! Now is our chance." I was steering the chair and was thoroughly over-excited and exhilarated.

She got pulled up once by the strongly swimming fish and struggled to get back under control but we were going back quickly along the trough and got right on top of the marlin and the leader was in hand.

But the fish was still too far away for a tag shot and it went off again, hounding and hounding away. The leader held and we crashed after it with it 3–4 metres away and leaping in our faces. It was spectacular.

We slalomed around, keeping right on its tail. The fish rolled and the tag was in.

It was a good striped marlin, fat and strong, easily 125kg and probably over 130kg.

It was the last action for the trip but what a result.

James had caught two marlin and, "third time lucky," his first legal one and also a champion kingfish at 30.6kg. (It sure looked a lot bigger).

Gemma had tagged two marlin, either of which would have been a new Female Junior World Record, if only we had known and had caught a new National and World Female Junior Record kingfish at 28kg.

The real triumph though, was that after having suffered the torture of the disqualified blue and the irony of losing out on the second fish due to a technicality, James could finally enjoy having a marlin to call his own!

"James was treated to a deserved heroes welcome, stood proudly by his 240 kilos of blue marlin and was thoroughly overwhelmed."

Three Broadbill And A Zoo Creature

I had never seriously fished for broadbill swordfish and I had never caught one either. You might say "obviously", but here in New Zealand some broadbill adventures are unplanned and accidental.

Some happen while deep bottom fishing for sea bass, hapuku or bluenose, or maybe even when fishing for marlin.

The fearsome tales of endless night-time battles might deter a lot of people from targeting broadbill, unless of course you happen to be a "longliner", anyway this was to be my first concerted attempt.

John Gregory, the owner and captain of *Primetime* had been expounding the virtues and fighting qualities of the " Gladiator", or "the Holy Grail", as he had put it. I didn't care too much as long as it didn't interfere with my main excitement of daytime fishing for marlin. Of course I had read and heard all the stories, including his dad's endless struggle for over fourteen hours only for the fish to get shark-bit by a lousy mako right at the death and even another guy's two shark-bit broadbill before eventually tagging a "toothpick" of forty kilos. A particular event that resulted in some understandable retribution on the sharks subsequently encountered on that trip.

It sounded like a lot of hard work and not a lot of fun.

Not like backing up fast through a following sea, chasing a monster blue or in the case of a hounding stripey, "wham bam thankyou m'am", fifteen minutes of heart-pounding pulsating, visual theatre, tag in, handshakes all round, can of beer, kiss of the lucky shirt and lures back in ready for the next pack attack.

No, no this meant drifting about in the dark in a bad sea, one hundred miles from the mainland, waiting to get beaten up by a zoo creature. No sleep, four layers of extra clothes and a great chance of getting very wet, or worse, if the battle scars on the stern of *Primetime* were anything to go by.

I had never been to the Three Kings before either. I had tried three or four times previously but the weather had always driven us back to North Cape and the shelter of Tom Bowling Bay and, for the moment, that intervening stretch of water, to me at least, seemed un-crossable.

It had in fact become a bit of a joke.

"Got your usual weather, John," the skipper would say to me the night before a trip.

This meant 20–25 knots, just what we were greeted with at the start of the previous attempt when we successfully fished the Whangaroa One Base Tournament instead. Then, low and behold, the following week

---

"my first sight of the Three Kings Islands was through thickening and descending cloud."

Primetime sailed off to the Three Kings for the New Zealand Nationals Tournament, in perfect weather, and broke just about every record in the book. During the course of a week on the Middlesex Bank they caught twenty-eight marlin and a broadbill swordfish.

"There, but for the grace of God, go I."

Well this time, damn the forecast, we were going anyway.

"Faint heart never won fair tart," was the way the skipper put it. All those years commercial fishing I suppose.

So it was, on the second morning after fishing up from Whangaroa the day before, we left Tom Bowling Bay and I was swollen with a wonderful feeling of expectation and barely controlled excitement.

I hooked-up on a smallish mako almost as soon as the lures had gone out and after tagging it we were on our way.

Some hours later my first sight of the Three Kings Islands was through thickening and descending cloud with it blowing hard and a huge double rainbow over North East Island. We had arrived via the King Bank, which

"with it blowing hard and a huge double rainbow over North East Island."

had been too rough to get near. With the wind against the tide, it was pretty grim.

So, it was overnight at anchor, up early to get live baits — boy those koheru "don't half hang on!" then off to the Middlesex Bank and plenty of daytime marlin and kingfish action, which you don't want to hear about because this tale is about broadbill — three broadbill to be exact.

Three broadbill all nice and complete without any tails missing or great chunks gone from the belly or in one case I'd heard of, no sword! — Bitten off!

Three broadbill, something that, as far as the Whangaroa Club's records show, had not occurred before in one season to one angler and something I now know can only happen at great pain and with no doubt a lot of good fortune.

We were on the broadbill grounds some miles west of the Middlesex Bank, a long way from the limited shelter of the Three Kings Islands and a long, long way from the welcoming calm of Whangaroa harbour.

It had just got dark, dinner was on the table, the squid baits were hanging lifelessly below their light sticks and the lucky blue balloons were dancing about in the breeze.

"Click!... Click! Click! Click!"

Four dinners were immediately deserted (as usual there was only the crew and myself onboard) and stations were quickly manned for action.

" I think he's got it! Maybe not, no, hold it, there is some weight I'm sure!"

"OK John, push up the drag and wind, wind, wind!"

I eased up the drag, got maybe half a turn on the reel and the rod heeled over hard and the line began to go off the reel, not fast like a marlin but steady and strong. By the time I was in the chair, buckled up and watching the line continuing it's departure into the night, the engines were running and the two other lines were nearly in. The fish didn't go too far, didn't go deep and seemed to follow the boat, albeit at an angle and under slight pressure.

So far so good, not too difficult, in fact a bit easy, maybe I could smooch it to the boat?

Oh Yeah? Any attempt to get any line or get the fish closer only resulted in fierce and violent head shakes which tore into my shoulder and neck muscles.

"Shoot! Better not do that again."

Whatever was down there now knew I was up here and it was not impressed.

A stalemate ensued which continued for thirty minutes or so, the fish was quite quiet and swimming with us but was hardly tiring itself out. The line was nearly straight down.

No matter how much I tried I couldn't get the fish to move an inch.

The captain called down from above. "OK John, get ready to lose some line."

I knew about this already from our blue marlin experiences. It was time to get the fish to work.

Fast circles around the fish to change the angle of the line, maybe get the fish off balance, make it swim and swim up and closer to the boat and more usually to get it really aggravated.

Away we went.

The chair was swung around to face the starboard and the line poured off against a lot of drag, we got a good angle and then wind, wind, wind, wind, wind, getting tight, drop the rod, pump, drop the rod, lift, WHOA! — My bum came off the chair and I hovered precariously, straight-legged, up on my toes, feeling the weight of the fish properly for the first time. By rolling my right shoulder and getting my weight back on my heels I plumped back in the fighting chair and was back under control.

Gradually everything settled down, I'd recovered a fair amount of line, all that was lost and some more. Then, off we went, circling again and again and again, the Dacron loop was back on the reel and there could only be forty metres of line out.

I could feel the weight of the fish nicely behind the boat with a nice angle and then it wasn't there anymore. The rod unloaded and I wound in the slack, the fish was gone.

One hour had passed as I wound in the bait.

It was completely untouched, but there, right up by the light stick the line was all crinkled up, like a spring. Bill-wrapped! Or should I say, sword wrapped! Shoot!

There was nothing else for it. We motored back to the start of the drift and put the same baits back in.

This time I was eating dessert. I remember it, blackcurrant cheesecake. I had a mouth full when the same rod with the same squid went off and I was at it again.

Don't eat cheesecake when you're fishing. You can't get rid of it when your mouth dries up; it's like chewing a pillow, even if it's swimming in fresh cream like mine was. Fruit salad would be better or ice cream but forget the cheesecake. Of course you might have a nice crew who ply you with liquid refreshment throughout your time in the chair, a crew who don't hide behind your back drinking tea, yawning and saying "Yeah, yeah that's it mate, keep winding, wind, wind, yawn, you're doing great, yawn. Another cuppa Johnno? Keep winding mate, that's it, yeah, yeah, yawn..."

240kg blue marlin bill on left, 191kg broadbill sword on right.

Well, initially, this fish acted the same as before except this time we got the going deep trick after half an hour, and with it the "God, my knees are killing me, my shoulder is seizing up," drop and wind, drop and wind, then the sulks and then the fast circles, circles which worked great for five or six times and then on the next, the fish rushed into the boat and all the line lost, remained lost.

"Bugger, these fish learn!" So I tried for ages to smooch the fish.

With the drag up and under a lot of pressure it had just fought back even harder, so I backed the drag off and the fish stopped running and just swam quietly with us and with some steady easing I managed to get the fish coming closer and closer into the boat. Whenever, however it began to get into the deck lights it dug in and wouldn't come any closer.

"If only we can get the leader and get a quick tag shot and cut the line quickly before it goes crazy."

We tried with the lights off but nobody could see anything and the idea was abandoned before the fish ran under the boat and cut us off.

"There is a lot more to this game than I thought. What the hell do I do now?"

Well I tell you what — back to the hard work and another couple of hours of the same.

Fish goes deep, stop him after 3–400 metres, fight the line back on the reel, then the fast circles, no rest for me or the fish, circles don't work. OK work hard, go to sunset, maximum pressure, try and get my bum back on the chair, then hold on with both hands as the line goes out again. Three hours coming up, three layers of clothes discarded and the underlying t-shirt is sopping with sweat and water from the hose, which has been cooling the reel and the roller guides and then, at last, I start to win.

The fish is coming up.

It's coming up and coming in.

"There's the double line, here comes the leader." I felt a renewed surge of energy.

All eyes searched the water for colour.

"Tuna bombs going in!"

I heard the call but what did it mean?

There were some small splashes just out of my sight out in the darkness, then "Flash, Whump! Flash, Whump! Flash, Whump!"

Both the flashes and the muffled explosions made me jump, and concerned, I awaited a reaction from the fish, which didn't come and then, there, I could see it in the water. Johnno slid open the door right in front of me and the other guy eased on the leader.

"Still got some boogie," cried the leader man, as a large flat black-blue sword appeared at the door six feet from my private parts and began slowly waving from side to side as if a white flag were attached.

"Gaff's in!" shouted Johnno as the sea foamed around my feet.

At this stage I felt it better to vacate the chair and easing back the drag I slipped back to a safer position as the still wagging sword was dragged onto the deck, not too closely followed by a fat silver-bodied fish with sparkling blue and bronze topsides and a huge, wonderfully coloured eye and it lay quivering on the deck. The body was seemingly pocked with small, almost circular holes and scars, caused by the aptly named but hideous cookie-cutter shark.

So there it was, eleven feet long overall with a three and a half foot sword, a tall proud dorsal and a wide strong tail root, no doubt providing much of the immense power it had demonstrated in the fight. We called it 175kg but knew that a lot of fluid would be lost from the strange-smelling body and loss of 10–15% body weight prior to getting onto the scales was to be expected.

I was delighted and thrilled to have won the battle, because that's what it was, a battle, there was not a lot of fun like the short visual sport you get with a marlin, this was pure combat, but what a feeling!

I was glad to lie down after a complete change of clothes and was even gladder not to get another bite that night; in fact I wasn't sure I wanted to do it again.

Something about the whole process disturbed me and I wasn't yet sure what it was.

However, the following night we were there again and sure enough we did not get to wait very long for the action to begin.

We all heard the reel go off for a couple of seconds and were on deck with the skipper up top looking down. There were three baits in the water and two of the lines had popped but nothing was happening. We, on deck, were looking towards the starboard side when the captain called down.

"Hey, what's that near the boat on the port side? Is that a light stick?"

I went to a rod, pushed up the drag on the reel a little and as I began to wind, right in front of me I saw another light stick thrashing from side to side and then take off. The line came up tight on the rod I was leaning on and it swung around under the pressure of the take and the line poured off the reel. I gradually eased up the drag some more and wished I had waited until I was in the chair as the weight of the fish made it difficult to get the rod out of the holder and get buckled up. In the meantime the other light stick reappeared.

We had got a double strike!

A double strike of broadbill, no less!

As luck would have it as I struggled to get organised and settle into the fight, the other fish which had not been struck, dropped the bait and the mate reeled back a squashed and mangled squid, having momentarily felt a tremendous weight on the line.

Well this fish was totally unlike the first broadbill. It took off and I couldn't do anything about it. We were forced to just follow as it led us, further out into deeper water. I knew immediately that it was a bigger fish and having planed up a dead blue marlin of 240kg earlier in the season I felt that I was dealing with a similar weight although very much alive.

Oh! The hopelessness felt when the line just peels off the reel and then the Dacron backing starts to disappear and the spool gets thinner and thinner and you know that it is going off 100 times faster than you can wind it back on again!

All I could do was to hang on to the base of the chair, lean back and wait for it to slow and hopefully stop.

There were no headshakes; no vicious thumpings on the rod, just immense weight and a steady pull gradually slowing. Then it was time for the agonising, sometimes only inch-by-inch, recovery of the line. Thank goodness for the twin speed Shimano Tiagra, trying to get a start in anything other than low gear would have been impossible.

Progress was slow, real slow, interrupted at times by a bit of a spurt from the fish and a loss of a few feet and then the relentless working it back up again. Once the Dacron was back on the reel and we were on the mono I pushed the drag up a bit more and we tried the fast circles which, after the first few goes when the fish became really agitated, began to work and the line was coming back well.

Then I heard what I didn't want to hear.

Oh no! Not now, not after all this work, not now it was getting close!

The skipper had seen the fin hunting on the surface, circling around as if trying to pick up the trail or maybe the courage to dart in to attack my struggling fish, which incidentally was not as defenceless as it might have been, as we were about to discover.

"I'll throw it a bait," shouted the mate and a large skippy-baited hook was soon hurtling away into the blackness.

"He's got it! He's got it! Feel this, you miserable bastard!" He struck violently, three, four, five times, each time jagging the hook hard into the shark's mouth making sure it was occupied with it's own safety and all thoughts of having a free feed instantly forgotten.

In the meantime as the mate was being dragged around the cockpit I was quietly going about my work and the fish was coming more easily until I was winding with little weight.

"It's coming up! It's coming up!" I informed everyone.

"Cut the shark off! Here comes the leader," called the skipper from his elevated position.

As he eased the boat forward I wound as fast as I could and the mate collected the leader and with tuna bombs going off all around it I saw a tail coming out of the night, followed by the almost motionless body of a big fish.

After only two hours the door was opened and the tail-wrapped fish was gaffed and hauled into the door opening.

However, it was too heavy and as it was coming backwards the pectoral fin and gill plate were getting stuck, so a line was run to the windlass and all of us got stuck in to get the fish aboard before any more sharks turned up.

With the fish on the deck and the door closed, all eyes fell upon our catch.

A big fish, twelve feet long and looking like 250kg, it was just about dead and its colour was beginning to fade to a steely grey.

No wonder it was a strange fight and no wonder it had succumbed at the end to the fast circles routine. Being hauled backwards was bound to do the job but it had meant that the fish was possibly more able to defend itself from the unwanted attentions of sharks.

I was sad to see it dead. Why do they have to fight to the death and why are so many seemingly foul-hooked? Why didn't the NZBGFC recognise 60kg tackle? (Although subsequently introduced.)

If I was to get to tag and release a broadbill a lot more thought was going to have to go into this. Thought by the *Primetime* team that would eventually produce a more effective method for catching broadbill swordfish than merely drifting subject to the vagaries of the wind and the tide. One that would produce more fish, very few of them foul-hooked and one that provides some visual excitement for the waiting onlookers.

I was to wait until the next trip on *Primetime* before I got the third broadie although four days after the capture of the second, when fishing aboard *Independence* with Captain Chris Ash (Crash to his buddies), I lost one from the same place and after a short fight when the double line snapped.

On this next trip I was accompanied by my new friend, Steve Waters,

Three Broadbill And A Zoo Creature | 63

"My third broadbill and the hardest and most painful three plus hours I had ever encountered."

or "Pom" as he is better known. Pom was along for the ride with video to record the action, be ready for a double strike and also to act as reserve deckie should I be able to put in place "a cunning plan" I had devised, that would see one of the deckhands in action and hopefully on the end of some of the same scornful abuse normally reserved solely for me.

In order that we would not be shorthanded and as I was not to be trusted with anything more technical than winding or writing a cheque, here was Pom, not exactly press-ganged, not quite sure what was in store for him but unable to turn down a six-day trip to the Three Kings. The fact that the weather forecast was crap did little to blunt our enthusiasm, as we were sure to get a couple of nice days.

Primetime was on 94 marlin for the season and I had also promised John Gregory the chair should we get to 99, so we bashed our way to North Cape with nothing to delay our progress and the next morning we had three different marlin hit the same lure one after another without the lure being fully retrieved and none of them stuck. (As it transpired I got four marlin for the trip and the boat was left on 98 and it was some weeks before the 100 was reached and passed and I think the skipper missed out on the thrill of boating the magic number himself). These fish hit us out on "the Compass Rose" and I failed to set the hook as the drag was not set correctly and the collective mood was a bit gloomy when we finally got to the Kings and it didn't improve when we couldn't catch many live baits once we got there.

Fishing is fishing however and the next morning we awoke to a wonderful day, flat calm and sunshiny, no wind at all and as we left for the King Bank, another boat was off to the Middlesex and the mood was lifting by the second. Each new day dawns with renewed optimism and expectation and this day we were to be rewarded for our faith.

During the day, I was lucky to tag three stripeys, all fat and feisty, the Middlesex Bank produced nothing although covered with baitfish and a boat fishing with us reported some recent broadbill action off the King Bank so that's where we stayed as the daytime excitement ended and the night-time version commenced.

The routine was different this time. There was zero wind, so drifting was out of the question and we slow-trolled a single squid at a couple of knots. How the hell was one tiny squid going to be found, at night, in the middle of the ocean, lightstick notwithstanding?

Well it was and in time this method was to be developed with spectacular results.

I had brought onboard some steaks from my second broadbill and we had feasted long and just before the cheesecake could appear, we got bit.

The fight started well, with the fish on top and close to the boat. It felt small and I was sure we were going to get it quickly and hopefully get a tag in it. For the first hour we had the Dacron loop either on the reel or out of the water. Backwards and forwards it went, like the rabbit on the dog-track it wiggled and waved, joyfully fixed to the line like the rabbit to its rail. We tried a fast circle but the fish rushed the boat immediately as if it had seen that trick before and we didn't try again. Then I tried to bully it and pushed the up on the drag as I was sure this fish was small. But it wasn't, nor was it impressed and it took off – downwards.

Down. Then down some more.

We had hooked-up in less than 200 metres but soon we were in 800 metres with the same amount of line out. I could make no impression at all and the more I pulled the more line the fish took, and so I eased back the drag in the hope that the fish would stop.

At first it didn't work and the calls from the cockpit were to tighten up again or all the line would be lost but it slowed and stopped and for a while we just followed. I noticed then that the angle in the line was changing slowly and after some seconds I realised that the fish was coming up.

"John, I'm getting some angle, I think it's coming up!"

It only takes minutes to get over 800 metres off the reel but getting most of it back took me an hour. Even with the fish coming up the belly in the line thus created, produced a great weight on the rod and just winding meant a slipping clutch with 28kg of drag, so pump and wind, drop and wind, countless times over and over until the Dacron was back on and the mono was filling up the spool.

Then, no weight!

I wound faster, cranking as hard as I could and the skipper ran the boat away and then we came up tight and everyone breathed a huge sigh of relief. Tight and heavy, the fish was up on top behind us and following.

Panic over.

Now was my chance and I leaned into the weight but it just kited out to the port side and I couldn't get it to come straight into us. What the

"Thank goodness for the twin speed Shimano Tiagra"

hell is going on here? In the third hour we got nowhere. Every time I started to get line and bring the fish in, it kited off to the port side or into the port corner and we had to get the boat away.

By now I was really tired and frustrated, I was in pain in my knees and my shoulders and my lower back.

This fish was beating me up.

For the first time the feeling of losing the battle came into my mind and I couldn't work out what to try next. The feeling of frustration grew and I began moaning and whining at everyone around me.

"Why does it keep running into the port corner, why can't I get this fish to the boat?"

"Could be foul-hooked?" offered the mate. "This could take a while." No doubt remembering a previous 14-hour struggle with the line half-hitched around a pectoral.

I had to regroup.

I knew I couldn't take much more, mentally I was buggered, I had made the mistake of assuming it was going to be a short and easy struggle and had given too much too soon. I resumed my complaining but we knew one thing and that was, as sure as eggs were eggs the fish would go to port, so on the next try, as it began to, the captain ran to starboard and spun the boat and I gained line as we backed up. A couple more and there was the leader; the fish was splashing weakly on the surface, the hook in a loose flap of skin on the right side of its belly.

No wonder it was going to port, with the hook in its side like that!

No wonder it rushed the boat when we tried the fast circles to starboard, the line was cutting into the side of the fish as the line came up its side and over its back!

I promise I had intended to release this fish and the tag pole was ready but I had taken such a beating and the frustrated red mist was still in my eyes, so when asked, "What do you want to do?" the words "Gaff the ****er" issued forth.

"My sentiments entirely," said Pom and the deed was duly done.

Like me the fish had little left and came onto the deck easily.

The hook came out simply and there were two long deep cuts down the right flank where the line had cut in when it was to our starboard. It looked 200kg and was fat and clean, with only a few small scars and a perfect sword, long and broad.

What a fish!

My third broadbill and the hardest and most painful three plus hours I had ever encountered. I couldn't contemplate having to fight another one for quite some time, so it was, when we got bit again only an hour or so later, I was able to introduce my "cunning plan".

Camera rolling, mate in the chair, buckled up and looking bemused and un-believing. "This is unreal, this ain't happening," he said as the fish zipped the line off the reel, straight down, in a very broadbill-like manner.

"Got your arse sucked onto the chair, mate?" asked Pom.

"I'm chewing me undies, mate, chopping washers!"

At last! The little bugger is in my hands. I am steering the chair and have the deckhose ready to cool down the reel and the roller guides, making sure of course that the monkey in the chair gets a good dose too.

Even the skipper gets in on the act. "How are your knots? Feeling confident about your splices?"

This is great! Payback time!

The fight was pretty one way. The fish took line against 30kg of drag and the mate, much of the time was straight up on his toes, leaning back and barely balanced and we followed.

The fish made for the bottom and stayed there, swimming out deeper and deeper into nearly 1000 metres until with nearly all the line gone the terrible task of recovery began, inches at a time.

On and on, hour after hour, the mate only resting to wash the deck with his own personal deckhose and to take a drink.

The night was totally, utterly calm, the mate, rising and falling in the chair, getting now one turn at a time, over and over again, causing the only ripple on the surface. There was nothing else for the rest of us to do but wait and as I waited, I thought.

I thought that maybe this wasn't such a good idea after all.

He's obviously attached to something a bit special, maybe a bloody world record! What would I make of that, I wondered? He's doing pretty well, in fact his technique is OK; he's taking his time and isn't too tired yet.

Blow this, what have I done?

So I left the chair to someone else and went upstairs to sulk with the skipper.

"Bloody big fish," he said, greeting me to the flybridge.

"You reckon?" I replied, mumbling something else to myself.

"For sure, we've never put so much weight on a fish before. I just hope the tackle holds up."

"Yeah, right. Let's hope the tackle holds up."

And hold up it did, right to the bitter end.

After three hours the Dacron loop came onto the reel and I was filming from the flybridge. Pom was nervously holding the gaff and the other mate was waiting for the leader to appear.

I say "the bitter end" as to some extent that's what it was because as the leader came onto the reel with the mate still winding, a massive tail appeared out of the calm sea, with the hook embedded in its end.

This tail kept coming and coming.

"Bugger, damn, bugger!" said the skipper mainly to himself. "It's a bloody big thresher."

And so it was. Bloody big.

More than 16 feet long, huge, massive, with a head four feet across and pectoral fins as big, it lay there wallowing on the flat surface. A desert sand colour on top and pure white underneath, I called it 400kg in the water.

"What's the world's on these, John?" the skipper was asked. "330 odd" came the reply after a while.

"Tag it," said the mate, "Let it go, tag it."

In fact he tagged it himself, the fish was freed, and as it continued to wallow, to all of us it appeared pretty much dead.

"OK, let's go back and get it," said the skipper as we began to drift apart.

But as we dropped back to reclaim this huge creature, it rolled and with one vast wave of its endless tail it was gone in the blink of an eye.

It had played dead.

"Thank Christ, I didn't have to put the gaff in it!" said Pom, "It would have gone berserk."

And so it would have.

In fact, I don't want to think about what might have happened.

It was a world record for sure and looking at the video I reckon I was nearer the mark at 400kg than the 300kg or whatever that was entered on the tag card.

"Without question, the biggest fish ever brought to the boat," said the skipper.

It had been a wonderful privilege to behold such a fish and after all my doubts, I was glad I hadn't had to fight it – but what if it had been a broadbill?

If You Don't Weigh It, Don't Say It.

The desire of my seventeen-year-old daughter Gemma was to dive the Great Barrier Reef, a dream she had held for ten years or more since snorkelling in the Bahamas when she was little. I made a deal that I would take her if she did well in her exams back in the UK where she was at boarding school. It must have been a sufficient spur because she passed and exceeded all expectations. So, whilst everyone was enjoying her success and all happy, especially her mum, I booked the trip to Cairns right at the height of the giant black marlin season in October. Three days live-aboard diving followed by five days live-aboard fishing. Well it's a long way to go for just three days, right?

The diving couldn't finish fast enough for me and with Gemma whining about how unfair it all was we climbed aboard the Cessna charter plane that was to take us up from Cairns to Cooktown and where the real excitement of the trip was set to begin.

We landed at Cooktown to find a deserted airstrip.

We stood amongst the kangaroos and waited.

Before too long a man came running along the track and I recognised him to be our skipper, Darren "Biggles" Hayden.

"Truck broke down, had to run the last mile, lucky I had my cellphone. Hi, I'm Biggles, you must be John and Gemma."

Biggs had come to collect us personally.

A replacement bus was brought out from the harbour and we bundled aboard for the fifteen minute bump over the dusty roads to where the

Allure was tied up and waiting for us. With no ceremony and little ado we were onboard, cast off and running 22 knots east to the reef and the fishing grounds three hundred metres outside Ribbon Reef Number 4 and in less than 80 metres of water.

On the way I discovered that the fishing had been good with a lot of fish of 800–950lb being reported and a few over the magic grander mark. The previous week had been the Lizard Island Tournament and the boat had released twelve black marlin and the winner over twenty. We were going to fish over the full moon when it tended to be a lot quieter but a possible time for the real biggies to show up.

We were not to be disappointed.

Other than Biggs, the crew was made up of Bo (Bozo the Clown) Jenyns reputedly one of the best wiremen in the world and Russ (Rasta) Housby, son of the late and great Trevor Housby; a man whose pioneering big game fishing in the Azores and Madeira had inspired me in the early 1980s. Young Russ and I knew many of the same fishing folk from the UK and Europe so reminiscences were interspersed with him rigging and fishing big tuna skip baits on one rod and smaller mackerel swim baits on the other.

A few baits were chopped off by wahoo or barracuda and one small "rat" black of 100lb or so mashed the mackerel swim bait, got bored and disappeared. Which was just as well as I'd forgotten the procedure of when to wind and when to freespool anyway, a fact that was soon to become evident.

There then followed a long period of burning sun and glare over blue water to die for in New Zealand, before out of nowhere a strike came on the swim bait.

The fish felt the drag when I was winding and not freespooling and dropped the bait. A new bait was quickly re-presented and low and behold the black marlin was there again, this time there was no mistake and it was hooked-up. My first black marlin of maybe 90kg (200lb) gave up fast on the ungainly 130lb outfit, which I was struggling to master, much to the horror of the crew.

"Need to work on your technique," muttered Bo as I slid out of the chair.

I had to agree with him, the winding hadn't been very pretty. However the first fish was on the board, even if it wasn't heavy enough to get the big rod working properly. I had got the feel of it all and after some adjustments to the harness and footrest I felt I would put on a better show next time. The deck crew however had given up on me as a bit of a disaster and I knew my critics would be on my back at the slightest provocation.

Later the time came for the huge run in of maybe half a mile and we were soon anchored in 12 metres of water behind Ribbon Reef Number 5 in the company of sweetlips and red bass.

After dinner that night, the talk was all fishing and the sharing of our various experiences of fishing throughout the world.

I told of the time on the King Bank north of New Zealand when the killer whales were nipping off the live skipjack tuna baits. This reminded Bo of the "rogue poofter seals" that did the same down Bermagui way. I wondered if, as in Monty Python, they were all named Bruce.

I told of the fat Yank in Jamaica who fought a big blue marlin for eight hours and as he lifted the rod for the final time for the fish to be leadered, the line touched the end of his long Cuban cigar and it was "goodnight Vienna". Rasta recounted the tale of the grander blue he leadered in Madeira after an epic battle and Biggs drank rum and gradually slipped into a coma.

The next day, after a leisurely start we went out maybe ten miles towing lures and at ten o'clock a big fish crashed the long corner and then hit the long rigger without getting hooked and just as quickly disappeared.

"Must've gone 800, maybe more, she wasn't lit up much but I thought we were going to get her, probably felt the hook the second time and decided not to come back". The skipper analysed the bite and we covered the same area for a while without raising anything else.

The suggestion is that the black marlin comes here at this time to spawn and that each big female is followed by a hopeful band of randy males, so when one fish shows there could be four or five around.

We continued with lures until nearly two in the afternoon when it was time to return to the reef for the afternoon bite and back to fishing the big dead baits.

Right on cue we got three bites resulting in one good fish being hooked-up and taking line. After one jump it showed itself to be around 200kg and the scrap began.

They like to get the fish in quick here, mainly because of the sharks, so after a fast and furious stripey-type fight with lots of hounding jumps and backing up, the leader was in hand but the fish was hooked high on its back down towards the tail and Rasta couldn't get its head up and it took off again, digging deep and feeling a lot heavier than 450lb. With over 25 kilos of drag and standing up straight-legged in the chair I knew it was shit or bust time. With both hands clamped on the spool, either the hook was going to pull or the fish was going to come up or do something different.

We were all grateful when the hook pulled because it could have gone on for another hour until both the fish and I were knackered, so it was a good result considering the circumstances. I was hot but not hurting, the fish was ready to fight another day and we were off again ready for another strike, which never came.

It was the day of the full moon and the fish were off the bite.

"So, how old are you then Russ?" I was interested to know.

"Twenty two."

"Get out of town!"

"How old did you think I was?"

"I dunno, thirty?"

"Thirty!"

"Well I never got girly tits and love handles 'til I was over 40."

"Dad! You can't say things like that to people!" interrupted Gemma.

"It's 900, it's 900. Look at her go!" yelled Biggs, shooting Allure backwards and the big fish was hounding away from us.

"Well, twenty two, must be puppy fat then."

"Don't worry Gem," said Russ taking two handfuls of belly and wobbling it about, "there's a lot of it, see? "

"Bloody hell! Impressive physique." Gemma's eyes rolled around in their sockets.

With the sun full in the sky to the west and the full moon in the sky directly opposite in the east, we ran back five minutes to our anchorage, dinner and an exchange of video action.

Great leaping Aussie blacks, including double hook-ups, versus Kiwi stripey and broadbill battles. Totally, totally different. On the one hand, blue, blue, warm, tropical water exploding with 800lb black marlin, lots of ocean on the deck, lots of smoke and lots of yelling. On the other hand, not so warm grey-green water in the darkness, woolly beanies, deckies pretending to be bored and a three-hour slog before a 420lb broadie is boated.

"Daytime is for fishing, nighttime is for talking about it," instructed Biggs.

"Do they really take the hooks out of those stripeys? Wow, he's holding the bill!" shuddered Rasta. "Did you see them get the hook out of the tail of that bloody big thresher? Crazy, man!"

"Not for me," insisted Bo. "Cut 'em off, I say. Those Kiwis are hard case loonies!"

"Bloody black would kill ya if ya grabbed its bill" informed Biggs, "But I fancy having a go at them broadbill!"

Then, more quietly, as an after-thought,

"Not in the dark though."

The third day began with snorkelling and the crew spear-fishing for coral trout. Gemma and I had a few close encounters with white tip reef sharks and one with a vast ugly moray eel with one of "Fluffy's" three heads. Not having "Harry's invisibility cloak" we plotted a course to scarper city leaving irritable "Fluffy" guarding his bommie.

Once we were all back onboard Biggs made a great call and decided to fish elsewhere.

So we steamed south for an hour before putting out the lures at Andersons Reef and towed down to the Agincourts.

Gemma put on the Bob Marley CD.

Immediately, at eleven thirty Gay Bob got bit.

I didn't see the fish hit the lure on the long corner but as I got in the chair and buckled up, I saw a five foot tail come out of the ocean like the flukes of a whale and beat the water to foam.

"It's a real big one!" yelled the skipper from on high, "Holy Mother, it's massive!"

With the other lines cleared, for once I was ready to go and we set off after the gigantic fish that was making a powerful run close to the surface.

"It's a grander and a big grander too!" Biggs could see the fish from his elevated position and kept me informed. As if I didn't know or couldn't tell that I was lashed to a steam train.

The fight was not what I expected. The big fish didn't have the same armoury of tricks as a blue marlin and unlike a broadbill it responded to heavy drag even if it was more drag than I had ever handled myself. The crew had told me that maximum drag was the answer to keep the fish up and hopefully jump itself to an early finish. This fish did not jump, instead it kept trying to get down and I was for most of the time standing up straight legged until the pressure came off and I could bounce on the chair and get a turn. This particular Penn 130 reel wasn't two-speed so it was high gear all the time and a real test to maintain line recovery against 28 kilos of drag or more. As usual there was a period of stalemate and Biggs got concerned about sharks so we had a bit of a fast circle to get the fish moving and hopefully planed up. I recovered the line lost in the procedure and we were running fast ahead and parallel to the fish with the line cutting through the water. If it had been a blue it would have been under the boat for sure but this black marlin slowed and the hard work began in earnest.

But all was not well.

The memory photographed in my head of the vast tail at the beginning of the fight came back to me and we collectively agreed that we had a tail wrapped or foul-hooked fish.

Not again!

It seems to be my fate to get the difficult ones to deal with. But hey, I was used to the long haul, as long as I could pace myself I would have a chance.

"Keep the pressure on, can you go with more drag? We have to get this fish fast, I don't want to lose it to the bloody sharks." Biggs was urging me to more frantic action.

So much for pacing myself.

The game was repetitive for a long time. The fish would have a bit of a spurt and I would pump it back, gradually easing the drag up and up each time, getting the line back and then waiting for a fresh move. All the time we expected the fish to jump with so much pressure on it but it never did and being tail wrapped maybe accounted for it.

Twice Rasta got the leader and everyone but me would get a good view of the fish before it spurted away again.

"Tail wrapped but hooked in the mouth," was Rasta's call that gave us some hope that at some stage it would get disentangled and we could get some weight on the right end of the fish.

As we approached the hour mark the fish made a monumental effort to get away and took nearly 100 metres of line against everything I could muster with one hand clamped on the spool and one hand clamped on the chair. I was teetering on the maximum the dodgy knees could take and as I began to lose heart and think I would have to ease off I was plumped back in the chair as the fish stopped, there was a lurch on the line and something happened.

As luck would have it the thing that happened was the thing we had hoped for.

The big girl had rolled or something and the line was off the tail and I was in business. Sensing that this was the moment, I pumped and wound as fast and as powerfully as I could until my head was pounding and the veins on my temples stood out like sleeping policemen. The fish had made its last major effort and I was now making mine. I was really hopeful of some acrobatics now and to get a good look at the massive creature I had been attached to for an hour but it didn't happen. I just kept going.

"There is the leader!"

One more wind, maybe one more, drop and heave.

"Grab it Russ, grab it like you never have, don't let go, give it everything. That's it, keep it coming. Look at the size of that thing!" Biggs was ecstatic.

With the fish leadered and alongside the boat the gasps of incredulity were emanating from all quarters.

"Oh Dad it is huge, so huge!" cried Gemma trying to get some snapshots around Russ and Bo who were both leaning into the leader.

I had already informed the crew that I had no intention of gaffing any fish, no matter what the size but if the boat wanted to weigh a big one then I was in agreement.

It was up to Biggs.

With Gay Bob recovered the skipper gave the call for the fish to be cut off and as the leader ran out I stood tall in the saddle to see a vast shape glide back into the blue and I felt at once disappointed at being denied the chance to look the giant in the eye and I was momentarily empty.

Bo said that Biggs and *Allure* had caught a number of grander blacks but had never weighed one over 1100lb.

"That was the one. If we had a mother ship or somewhere to run into I would have taken it. That was the biggest fish we ever brought to the boat." Biggs was staring out over the blue water.

Russ had leadered his biggest ever fish, I had got my first grander and Bo must have got some good video footage for us to drool over later.

"Sorry John, no video, numb-nuts Bozo dropped the camera at the start and it won't work, we got nothing." Russ gave me the bad news.

If only it had jumped.

But I could still see that tail, like a whale.

Hey, so what, it had ended the way I wanted, both the fish and me were still swimming and there was still time for some more!

Bob Marley had done it again.

We spent a while talking about the possible size.

A fish had been weighed at 1170lb or thereabouts, which had a short length of 12 feet 3 inches and a girth of 6 feet 6 inches. The recognised method of judging the weight of most gamefish is to square the girth, multiply by the short length, (from the tip of the lower jaw to the fork of the tail) all in inches and divide the total by 800. The estimates on my fish suggested a depth of at least 3 feet 6 inches, complete with a fat "double belly" and a head that looked "small", a sure sign of a big fish. So, 1200? 1300? As they say "If you don't weigh it, don't say it!"

It didn't matter, we all knew what we had seen and done and the satisfaction was overwhelming.

Gay Bob, the Hawaiian Lunger lure with the Ocean Lure Concepts "Gai Bob" skirts, was saluted by all and carefully placed back in the lure box and we were back to towing deadbaits for the afternoon bite.

A small black marlin appeared behind the big skipping tuna and for fifteen minutes or more we tried to get it hooked-up. It hit the tuna a couple of times but it was just too big for it to eat. We pulled the smaller swimming rainbow runner over in front of it but this fish was preoccupied with the big bait. Once it lit up and tore in but we knew it was to be to no avail and after changing baits the fish disappeared.

Like previous days it was then quiet until at four in the afternoon things went crazy.

First the swim bait got nailed when nobody was paying attention.

A fresh bait was immediately run out and a big fish absolutely crashed the big tuna on the other rod. This marlin of around 350kg flew through the air completely out of the water and smashing the bait without hooking up. A fresh tuna was run out and was immediately nailed by another fish that appeared to be hooked-up as the line was screaming out and the *Allure* was powering ahead. I struggled to lift the rod out of the holder in the covering boards and horror of horrors the drag was pushed way up beyond strike at over 25kg of drag. The effect was to pull me straight back into the transom where I clung to the rod, fighting not to be pulled overboard. I had a hairy time trying to get back into the chair, get the rod in the gimbal and pull back to get the harness buckled up. All the time Bo was screaming instructions at me. It was a nightmare!

I was totally out of control from start to finish and it was no surprise when the fish jumped and spat the bait as I fumbled with the gears trying to wind.

So as fishing does to you all the time, a day that had started so wonderfully well, ended down the pan.

"Bo got a bit excited there Gem," I said on the way in.

"Dad, he looked as though he wanted to rip off your head and spit down your neck."

"So, 1200? 1300? As they say 'If you don't weigh it, don't say it!'"

"Mmm, he'd have to stand on a box," was my measured reply.

All in all I was glad to get to the anchorage and start on the rum and contemplate the day's events.

Whilst we had been having our late afternoon disaster, two other boats beside us had hooked-up. One lost their fish to sharks and the other got spooled chasing a fish they couldn't keep up with. At least it wasn't just me that was shown up and for once the big one had not gotten away. What a day!

At anchor, the previous night's viewing came to mind and I spent some time considering the similarities between giant black marlin fishing and everything else I had done previously, including broadbill fishing and concluded that there were none.

As usual fishing had thrown up an entirely new experience and a surprising one at that.

Fishing is full of "tricks". Some for the angler and many more for the fish.

Putting more drag on a pulling broadie seems to make them pull more; they have immense power.

Stopping one, when it is digging deep with a lot of line out, could be as simple as easing the drag right back and marvell when the fish starts to cruise back up.

A light drag ain't the order of the day on these Cairns, blacks.

As much as you can stand and more was what I was advised in order to bring them up. With luck, all the action can be performed pretty close in with the fish never too far away and on the top shot after the initial hook-up and recovery. There is not much tagging done and maybe only in tournaments and the hooks are left in the fish. Sharks are such a big problem the deal is to get them in and away, Kiwi stripey-style only three or four times the size.

But I had to think of a better way of getting to the chair with at least 20kg of drag on the heavy 130lb outfit. Man Mountain I ain't! And I also wanted to see more of the fish!

Something I need not have worried about because I was going to be seeing quite a bit soon enough.

Yet another leisurely start on day four and the baits were in the water at 0930. We had spent the night at the St Crispins Country Club.

St Crispins Reef is like any other but according to Bo, if you get laid here you get a t-shirt printed "St Crispins Country Club". Needless to say I gave no cause for the printers to get excited but the snorkelling was great and the water was warm and "clear as" and I couldn't think of many nicer spots to work on a t-shirt.

Do you think you both get one?

What happened next was pure joy and could not have gone more to plan.

We were fishing a slightly smaller scaly mackerel with a smaller hook as the skip bait and accordingly the strike drag was set slightly less. I had informed everyone that my plan was to ease back the drag once the fish was hooked so I could get to the chair without incident but as things turned out it wasn't necessary.

A marlin appeared behind this skip bait and nailed it all lit up and full of intent. It did not get the hook and the order came to wind the bait back up and then the shout,

"Freespool! Freespool!" from the flybridge, and "He's got it, drag up! Drag up!"

Performing like a veteran I smoothly did as bid and the boat powered away and the line poured off the reel.

In the chair and buckled up the fish was the perfect black marlin. Jumping and jumping, headshaking and hounding away in a manic fury. We were fast on its tail and I was cranking like a good 'un. It made a desperate attempt to sound but I was quick on the drag and stopped it before it could get going, it was up again and we were on it like a cat on a mouse. After only a furious five minutes Russ had the leader and I got Bo to stick a tag in it and cut it away. The fish, probably 250lb and none the worse for our brief encounter off Opal Reef, feeling its freedom, shot off over the surface to wild applause and a satisfying feeling all round of a job well done.

"Wow that was great! Just perfect!" I felt good.

I should have known that it couldn't last.

Other than a fish that came and inspected both baits before tailing off along the swell it was dead until, not long after 5pm, it hit the fan. Big time!

Maybe it was because we had gone so long for nothing, although I knew we had approached the witching hour it had remained quiet and there wasn't long left in the day.

Bo was still pacing the deck with his usual pedantic intensity, wound up and patting his sunglasses with his left hand as if they were continually falling off; a trait that amused Russ and myself and we would do the same behind his back.

I always fish in shoes, after once slipping on the footrest when backing up and everything was wet and slippery and I dented my shins. It wasn't really necessary on *Allure*, as they had glued skateboard grip on the footrest (like coarse sandpaper) and it worked well. Anyway, for some dumb reason I had just removed my shoes when we got bit on the big skip bait.

The rigger popped, the drop back ran out but the fish didn't take line. I began to wind the bait back up.

"Wait," advised Bo.

So I wound some more.

"WAIT!" screamed Bo.

So I wound some more.

"WHAT ARE YOU DOING?!" Bo was apoplectic. He was purple!

"You used the "W" word," I shouted back.

I kept winding and the fish grabbed the bait and tore off with it, the reel screamed and the boat powered ahead.

What happened then was unreal.

With the rod out of the holder the weight of the drag pulled hard on the rod, which I was prepared for.

What I wasn't prepared for was the safety line.

The safety line came up between my toes and was forced in tight by the weight of the drag on the running fish. My right leg was whisked

---

"Bo (Bozo the Clown) Jenyns reputedly one of the best wiremen in the world"

from under me and I crashed onto the deck gripping the rod in one hand as though my life depended on it. Bo helped me up and into the chair and unbelievably the fish was still on. As it came up to jump and throw itself about I began to wind like a madman and the boat started to back up. But, and in this tale there are a lot of buts, in the fall I had knocked the reel into low gear and I was winding and getting nowhere. At this point the fish came clear out in front of me, the line was slack and it threw me back the remains of the bait.

I have always said that there are lucky fishermen and fishermen with no luck.

I know I'm a lucky fisherman but having luck cuts both ways, good and bad, you just have to take it as it comes and expect the best and worst of both.

I won't recount the post mortem; I will only say that it wasn't a happy crew that returned to the "Country Club" immediately thereafter.

I was cut and bruised and not in receipt of any sympathy.

But hey! Tomorrow is another day! Sod 'em.

I awoke on our last morning to the sound of a longliner skipper talking over the SSB to what was probably a charter boat; I could only hear one side of the conversation.

What he said was mind-boggling. He told of having his gear wrecked by a significant quantity broadbill (if I told you how many, you wouldn't believe it) and having to take two days to repair it. He told of blue marlin being everywhere and him cutting off 350kg fish and of big-eye and yellowfin tuna being bitten off at the gills by pilot whales. He told of one set that came in only tuna heads and blue marlin bills and that the "bloody whales" were following him everywhere and if it wasn't them it was the white sharks.

What was more, it all been happening less than thirty miles off the reef.

Wow, this Cairns fishery is some place.

Biggs said, like all skippers do, "It don't pay to leave fish to find fish." So after another snorkel and a leisurely start we were back out and fishing down the Linden Bank in search of another big black marlin to round off the trip.

The day was slow with only wahoo and tuna about for us to show some interest in. We even tried fishing live skippies. This was my turn to have a laugh. Bay of Islands-style it sure wasn't and the baits were either dead or nearly dead by the time they were back in the water and spinning. The circus was curtailed abruptly and we were back to a skipping scaly mackerel and a swimming rainbow runner.

Not long after 4pm and it was bite time!

Even if I had never caught the big, big one it would be this next fish that I would remember, as it put on the most spectacular display and demonstrated the most perfect example of what this place is all about.

The big scaly mackerel was absolutely engulfed by the fish as it hurtled across the swell, broadside and in full view. The hook-up was instantaneous, everyone saw the same thing at once and we screamed out together.

"FISH!"

"It's 900, it's 900. Look at her go!" yelled Biggs, shooting *Allure* backwards and the big fish was hounding away from us. Each leap bringing loud cheers from all of us as I watched the line disappear off the reel and easing up the drag all the while until I began to lift off the seat of the chair.

Even with 24kg of drag on the strike I had got to the chair easily and unaided and had been ready for action.

The fish continued to skip over the swells leaping at least a dozen times before the weight of the drag began to tell and it slowed, only to rear up like a cruise missile and stand on its tail shaking its head furiously before sinking down vertically and then performing the same wonderful stunt twice more almost in slow motion.

We knew this was our chance and I recovered line faster than ever until my right arm was complaining and the warning voice in my head was screaming "enough". Still I kept cranking and blotting out the pain and the voices until I thought my head would explode. I tell you strenuous activity in 36 degrees and 100% humidity is not to be recommended to the over-fifties.

The fish came out again, much closer this time and it was lit up by the westering sun and it shone like a vast steel bar as it hung there before crashing back and disappearing in a surge of white spray.

It tried to sound just as we got on top of it and up went the drag as far as I dared and I clung on for all I was worth. The fish came straight back up and ripped away from us, tearing over the surface and taking 300–400 metres of line in a heartbeat. We chased as fast as I could reel and it continued to leap, looking every ounce of 900lb. I couldn't believe that it could keep this up and that it must burn itself out with such an amazing display but it made one more effort that proved to be its downfall. It turned 90 degrees, not malevolently blue marlin-style but just a fresh move to try something different and we sped to cut it off with me winding like crazy again. We were quickly on top of it and with the drag over 30kg and holding on for all I was worth the fish tried another run but I held it and got a couple of turns on the bounce. It tried again but with the same result so it came up, saw the boat and dug in. For a moment we both awaited the others next move and before it could make another dig I went nearly to sunset and held the chair with both hands, to the anguish of the crew and put everything into getting her up. As my legs began to wobble the fish gave in and as I dropped to the chair I slipped the reel into one to one and it was drop and wind drop and wind until Russ could snare the leader. With the double and plenty of wind on leader back on the reel Russ got a couple of good wraps and as Bo cut the leader above Russ, I put the rod in the chair and slipped out to see my prize.

Its tail was near the surface and it had its head down and thumping to get away. I got a good look before Russ couldn't hold on any longer and the leader slipped through his hands and the big fish powered away and down and into the blue.

Twenty minutes of full on, heart-pumping, head-pounding action. It definitely doesn't get any better than that! That was simply the best!

There was only half an hour left, if only we had stopped fishing at that moment.

"Wow, Dad that was amazing, but that was a puppy in comparison to the real big one. That was twice the size; I got some great video though. What a fight." Gemma was flushed with excitement.

I went inside and ran my head under the cold tap and sunk a couple of beers. I needed time to recover.

However, the baits were back out and we got bit again. I wasn't ready and screwed up the freespool.

A fresh bait went out and we got bit again. A fish about 200kg grabbed the big skip bait and dropped it.

"Wind, wind, wind," urged Biggs, and the fish grabbed it again.

"Freespool! Freespool!"

I planted my left thumb on the spool and threw the drag lever into freespool and being surprised by the sudden effect it had and unsure of how much pressure to apply, the reel started to overrun before I could get both thumbs on the spool. With the near backlash cleared and winding down we were amazed that the fish was still on but just as we were about to power forward to set the hook the fish jumped and spat back the bait, all head and backbone of it.

With Bo looking at me as though I was playing the prat version of Rimmer and Biggs about to launch into one of his speeches, I waved them off and collapsed on the day bed.

The trip was over and we started the thirty-mile run back to Cairns.

Five days, five fish, one monster and one monster's mum, what a trip!

We said our goodbyes to Biggs, Bo and Rasta.

The Aussies give everyone a nickname.

I dread to think what mine is.

"The desire of my seventeen-year-old daughter Gemma was to dive the Great Barrier Reef"

The Mission

Part 1 – "Paying My Dues"

The big game fishing season in New Zealand doesn't get under way much before January even though yellowfin tuna and the odd striped marlin are regularly caught in December.

Like others, I felt that, weather permitting, fish could be caught earlier, broadbill for sure and even black and blue marlin had to be about somewhere, it was just a case of going out and finding them. The blues had to get to Waihau Bay from somewhere, probably from the north or east, so it meant studying the SST charts (sea surface temperature), watching the movement of the East Australian Current and listening out for the "stories" from the commercial boys. I had set my heart on catching a big blue marlin in New Zealand so an early pioneering trip, out wide, maybe from Auckland was put on the front burner.

The season being quite short in New Zealand, January to June being the realistic limit, the winter is therefore long and unbelievably tedious. Not being NZ-bred, snapper and bottom fishing in "tinnies" is not my cup of tea so a trip to Vanuatu for some mahimahi and wahoo and one to Cairns for the big "Blacks", helped break up the decided gloom but by November I couldn't stand it any longer and the thought of another two months inactivity was unbearable.

With the big game boats either out of the water and the crews pig hunting, baby sitting, crocheting or whatever they do in the off-season, or watching the "W.I.F.I.s" ponce about on the Hauraki Gulf chasing some "Cup" or other, I had to wait until *Primetime* was done with it's maintenance.

Not that skipper John Gregory was content to be waxing and polishing, he was as desperately keen as me to get out and prove a point. After all he'd done it the year before when, with the competition rugged up in front of the fire, he'd captured huge broadbill in the middle of winter, even if he did have to press-gang the anglers onto the boat.

So once the big boat was done with it's sea trials and looking better than new we didn't delay in getting a plan in motion. The weather had been reasonably settled for a while and it appeared we were in with a chance of getting seven or eight calm days on the trot, that were favourably conducive to an offshore mission. It was apprehensively but with high expectations and that wonderful optimism with which all fishing begins, that we got under way from Westhaven, Auckland in mid-December.

Last minute problems had delayed our start but there had been no reports of any fish being seen recreationally, so we hadn't missed anything. The commercial boys had found blacks and stripies on their longlines and the week previously a lot of skipjack tuna had been netted but the warm water, in which they had been found, had disappeared in the strong westerlies we had been getting. The SST maps had been showing warm water outside the Poor Knights Islands and north-east of North Cape but it appeared that colder water had been blown over the top of it and what was 20°C degrees was now down to 18°C.

The initial plan was to check out some spots outside Great Barrier Island and then move up to the Knight's Terrace and beyond.

With me was my twelve-year-old son James and he was sulking miserably having discovered that his mum was planning to take the rest of the family to see the new **Harry Potter** and the new *Lord of the Rings* whilst we were away and we weren't planning to work our way back to our home port of Whangaroa much before Christmas.

"Come on Bud, cheer up, we might even find you a broadbill."

"Go away, leave me alone. Can we go back now?"

"We are going back, just might take a week or two to get there, that's all."

"I hate you, you're the worst father in the world. You made me come out here; I'm going to make your life miserable. I promise I will!"

"Hey! Look, America's Cup boats!"

"Shut up! That won't work. Go away! You're probably lying anyway."

I was, so I went away.

I should have brought his sister, miserable little bugger.
Who'd rather go to the movies than go marlin fishing?
Most kids I suppose. Oh well, too late now.
I looked for encouragement elsewhere.
"Hey Matt! What do you reckon? Plenty of fish?"
"Too early mate. I don't like fishing before February. This is a total waste of time."
"Do you like going to the movies?"
"Eh?"
"Never mind"
What a misery! This could be a long trip.

Before sailing we'd helped the captain buy the stores at the New World near Westhaven; he'd taken a fancy to the banana pies. Mike, in charge of the galley, had looked dubiously at them when they came aboard.

"Better eat those buggers quick," was all he said.

I remained cheerful and confident, no amount of bad omens were going to spoil my fun.

After the first day of bottom fishing and the crew diving for crayfish off Great Barrier Island we finally waved goodbye to The Needles, put the lures out and made our way out and up the coast towards the Knights Terrace.

We towed lures for ten hours and it was good to see some old friends getting a good wash, plus some less familiar ones, introduced to the pack by the newest crewmember and lure maker, Mike Harris.

"What's that pink and purple thing supposed to be?"
"Never you mind, that's caught thirteen marlin," stated Mike proudly.
"Thirteen? You sure it's not scaring them off?"
"You won't say that when it gets you a 400 kilo blue." Mike's prickles were in evidence.

"Everyone's a bit touchy; I seem to be treading on a few toes." I thought to myself.

So I went up top to see the skipper, who was in the process of washing down a pill of some sort.

"Heart pill." He said jokingly, answering my unasked question.
"Heart? Too late to try and grow one now."

Luckily, right on cue, the Shimano alarm sounded before I got savaged and I fell down the stairs and pushed the drag up on an albacore and our first gamefish of the season was duly dispatched for dinner.

The day wore on and we continued working towards the Poor Knight's Islands and past the spot where we got our first two marlin earlier in the year on January 5th, a small striped marlin and James' 240 kilo blue. Undisturbed but undaunted we moved out to the old broadbill grounds for a drift.

The squid came in untouched at dawn. The lures went out again and we trolled towards the Cavalli seamount and the start of the "60 mile ground". The 60 mile ground is a favourite area of the skipper and where a lot of big blue marlin had been sighted early in previous seasons but the weather often prevented a sustained assault on these fishing grounds, which were relatively unexplored by game fishermen.

The water temperature began to drop as we got out deeper and it looked grey and lifeless. Before long an alarm sounded.

The starboard motor shut down and as it was stuck in gear, it couldn't be restarted. After telephone consultations and unsuccessful efforts to resolve the fault, we turned back in to Tutukaka. An engineer was on his way from Auckland and running gently on one engine, our arrival coincided with his.

The problem was resolved by the replacement of a faulty control unit.

The captain, muttering to himself and grumbling about double time and travelling expenses, took the opportunity to top up with fuel and later in the afternoon, with the problem fixed, we ran straight back out to the Poor Knights and made a few circuits around the area where some hapuku fishermen had recently hooked up on a marlin on 15 kilo gear only to lose it at the boat when the line snapped because they had no leader to hold on to.

We found vast schools of blue mackerel, all over an area, ten miles outside the Poor Knights. The aerial spotters had seen them and via the radio we could tell that the big purse seiners were on their way to clean them up.

We pulled the lures and left the area just before dark and ran through the night back on course again for the Cavalli seamount and through the cold barren water we had seen earlier in the day.

By dawn, as we got closer, the water temperature began to rise and the colour got bluer and bluer. It was looking good.

The sun was strong and the sea was calm and beautiful. I was still

The Mission — Part 1 – "Paying My Dues"

excited, keen and full of optimism and expectancy.

Just one shot, that's all I wanted.

Any minute now.

Albacore were coming thick and fast and James was having a ball on the bungy line.

"His mum will be happy." I thought. "She loves albacore."

I watched the small lure on the bungy line as it danced in the prop wash, constantly ducking and disappearing and wavering in the flow. The line straightened and the bungy stretched and plunged down rapidly. Before James could grab the line, or the boat could slow, the rubber bungy sprang back loosely.

James pulled in the line but the fish was gone and so were the lure and the leader.

"That was no albacore," said the captain. But, unseen, the culprit remained unknown.

A new lure was employed but regardless of all our suddenly revitalised

"the skipper had a bit of fun with James and I by getting us to drag bluenose out of 350 metres of water."

attention, nothing else appeared. So we moved on to the Whangaroa seamount.

The wide channel between the two was full of water that was green and cold but as we approached the next seamount it shot up to over 20°C and it was "blue as"; clear and tropical, it looked perfect.

Right on top of the seamount in 700 metres there was a huge school of albacore ready to commit suicide and we worked round them for the rest of the day without raising a thing remotely resembling a big blue marlin on the marlin lures, but twice more an unseen assailant smashed off the bungy line, much to the consternation of the captain.

At dark, it was out with the squid, which was getting whiter and whiter, and another undisturbed night's sleep.

There was no wind at night and the boat barely drifted a couple of miles. I lay on my bunk with my hands folded behind my head and listened to the gentle slapping of the ocean against the hull and the blowing of the whales as they cruised around and inspected us.

"Where are they?" I said quietly. "Where are the damned stick-faced things?"

"You shouldn't call them names, Dad," said James, rightly admonishing me.

"Tomorrow is decision time, Jamesy."

Do we continue west and around to the Gobey Bank or go further north to look at the three seamounts known only to the commercial boys? These areas are 100–120 miles offshore and there was a lot of deep barren water to cross whichever way we went. The SST showed warm water on the Gobey Bank but cold to the south of it so it would be a long run fishing through green cold water to get back towards the Three Kings. We still hadn't had more than five knots of wind and there might not be another chance to go out wider.

"The Kings can wait."

So, the next morning, we turned our back on New Zealand and sailed into the blue yonder.

It was magnificent. The fishing grounds were amazing with canyons, guts and seamounts. The sea temperature went up to 22°C and it was a calm, oily tropical blue but it was barren.

No bait, no albacore, no whales, no nothing!

Just one shot, that's all I needed, just one gigantic blue marlin to monster one of Mike's scarecrows and do the haka.

I waited and watched and waited and watched some more.

James had retired to his Gameboy, the miserable deckhand was smirking in his cabin again, the lure maker was checking his babies and the captain's jaw set firmer with each passing and uninterrupted hour.

I knew he wouldn't give up, so I waited and watched some more, scouring the expanse of featureless ocean, searching for the smallest clue; a sign.

"Just one shot."

That night we let the squid out over a big gut that just screamed "swordfish" but to no avail.

Three nights and not even a shark, not even a blasted blue shark.

"There has got to be a marlin here somewhere!"

And there was.

The next morning Mike put the lures out early.

At 0645 in 1400 metres of water, in the middle of nowhere, a striped marlin appeared in the gear, all lit up and quivering.

It wavered behind a lure and swayed over to another and hovered tantalisingly.

The roar from the skipper was enough to scare it away and it sank out of sight.

The excitement was not enough to keep the idle deckhand from his bunk and the rest of us slipped back into a coma and we fished our way back in towards the coast.

I wondered how many times there had been unseen "lookers" inspecting the lures only to quietly slip away again unnoticed. The thought kept me hoping.

"Just one shot, come on. Just one."

For two more days we followed the same pattern, we towed lures all day over the likely spots and soaked a squid all night. The water was blue and warm there were good current lines and there was bait. We did the Knights Terrace again and then worked a line closer in and up to the seamount off Whangaroa and the 505, then around the spot off Berghans Point where we tagged the big 300 kilo plus blue marlin in the Whangaroa One Base Tournament back in February and then out to the "Garden Patch" off Cape Karikari.

We approached and fished around a bluenose drop-liner, just about the only other boat we had seen for days, he'd had a marlin near his boat, he'd advised our captain on the radio.

"We had travelled 1200 nautical miles, the weather had been brilliant, the sea magnificent"

Now the ocean never fails to amaze. We had seen a lot of things on this adventure, some that were marvellous and even heart-warming, such as pods of dolphins with the babies, barely a metre long, leaping in unison with their mothers; some that were strange such as leaping sunfish and leaping manta rays; some awesome such as humpback whales sporting and broaching around us at night; some, on other more successful trips, exciting and thrilling such as marlin or yellowfin tuna crashing through the bait schools.

But some things – well, some are just totally shocking.

Things that only serve to confirm the ocean to be a place where life and mainly death is played out with a ferocious intensity albeit mostly below the surface and out of sight of human sensibilities.

A pod of dolphins had been playing around the drop-liner for some time as the commercial fishermen retrieved their lines.

A pod of orcas turned up and began feeding.

Feeding on the dolphins.

On a different occasion I was playing a striped marlin of about 130 kilos when it attempted to jump. It was half out of the water when a great white shark bit it clean in two. The remaining half, with the bill and head, slipped slowly back to disappear in one more bite.

You don't contend with forces of nature like these, they just happen, but I reckon we're just not supposed to see them. We're not supposed to see live sharks being finned either but of course we know that goes on and maybe it is resultantly not as shocking, leaving the brute force of the natural world to win hands down.

That night, for once, we ran in to North Cape and put down the anchor.

The next day we fished back to the Garden Patch and worked it all day save for a couple of hours when the skipper had a bit of fun with James and I by getting us to drag bluenose out of 350 metres of water.

We stayed out for the night's squid swimming before towing back the next day to Stevensons Island and home.

We had travelled 1200 nautical miles, the weather had been brilliant, the sea magnificent, we had found plenty of bait but other than the one "looker", we'd had no strikes, no hook-ups and no captures, in fact "All Zeroes".

"You've paid your dues on this trip," said the smirking deckhand as we left the boat on Christmas Eve.

"Paying's all I have done," I muttered, thinking ahead to nine days time when we would be off again for seventeen days and I'd be paying some more.

The Mission

Part 2 – "Zoë, Zane And A Zebra"

Between Christmas and the New Year Cyclone Zoë had reared it's miserable head and attacked some of the remote Pacific Islands between the Solomans and Vanuatu. As we sailed on *Primetime* from Whangaroa on the 3rd of January it looked as though Zoë was looking for more substantial fare as it moved south.

Hopefully it would pass west of New Zealand and fizzle out.

We went up the coast anyway, the only place we hadn't checked out so far were the Banks east and north of the Three Kings and I was still looking for a blue marlin. If we picked up any stories on the radio we could always turn back, we had seventeen days to play with!

We set course for the Garden Patch where we had found good water before Christmas.

It was green but loaded with skipjack tuna, the first we had seen and a good sign as long as the commercial boys' aerial spotters didn't find them. They were still working the mackerel between the Poor Knights and Great Barrier and also on the west coast after the albacore.

In the middle of Doubtless Bay and out of nowhere we got a bite, the left rigger popped and the line ran out.

I was alone this time, all children preferring the delights of the surfboard and the beach. Whatever turned up on this trip would be all mine.

On settling down the fish was coming in easily, too easily.

" I can see the lure," called the skipper from on high, "you sure you've got a fish on?"

"No, not really." I continued to collect the line.

All eyes scanned the surface. Maybe it was weed?

But with a quick flash of neon our first billfish of the season was coming to the boat.

A shortbilled spearfish!

The first one I'd caught, in fact the first live one I'd ever seen.

"Tag it! What a magnificent looking fish!"

It was called 15 kilos, tagged, admired for it's brilliance and released unharmed.

Spirits raised we pressed on, Cyclone Zoë was 140 miles north west of New Zealand and moving slowly; two days later it would be in the same place but we weren't to know that.

We continued northwest to find the warm water we had seen on the SST and found it eventually in 1500 metres. It was 20°C as expected but green, which wasn't.

There were whales and hundreds of gannets and albacore everywhere, as far as the eye could see. Dolphins poured in on the boat like apaches attacking the wagon train and we worked the area relentlessly, all the time moving on to the area north of the King Bank but it remained green

"accepted the tag, lay quietly while the hook was removed, lit up it's stripes like a zebra and swam off strongly"

and the temperature began to drop.

I constantly looked ahead, expecting to see the weather coming but there was no front in evidence.

Where on earth was Zoë?

We turned southwest to come down the eastern side of the King Bank, planning to anchor at the Kings for the night. We could afford to lose a day if necessary whilst Zoë buggered off.

Even with only five knots of wind the Johnson Trough was as rough as guts in the strong tidal flow and as we got to the southern edge of the King Bank we got the weather forecast.

Zoë was not going to bugger off, it was heading southeast and about to descend upon us.

We could stick around and ride it out or we could run back to North Cape.

Time for "Plan B".

I made the call and we ran back to North Cape through the evening and passing through 16°C water all the way.

By dawn, the next morning, Zoë still hadn't turned up.

We ran around the Cape and fished down to Cape Karikari. At 0830 we got a bite on the short corner in 140 metres of green water. The "Big Rat" had taken a hit.

None of us had seen the bite but it was a marlin.

It didn't jump and we were concerned.

I worked the fish, as gently as I dare, all the way to the boat, putting as little weight as possible on it to keep it near the surface. We didn't backup fast and I just collected the line, daring not to change the angle on the fish. I tried to keep the weight off and to be smooth and steady but the swells were hard to read and as the Dacron loop appeared the fish hung heavily in the swell, just as the captain nudged the boat into forward gear. A few metres of line slipped off the reel and then, Ping!

The line leapt back towards me and I wound in the slack. The whole leader was milked up where it had been wrapped around what was obviously a big fish.

I was gutted. "Sick as a parrot."

A marlin had taken a shot at the big blue marlin lure in the big blue marlin position.

The skipper guessed "black".

We shall never know.

For the next two days we worked the area around Cape Karikari in heavy rain.

Zoë had slowly but finally arrived and seemed to be pleased to be here.

It rained torrents. Straight down and endlessly in torrents of warm water.

But then Zoë did a strange thing.

It moved west.

I knew what would happen. Zoë was going to come back.

After the tropical downpour we were greeted by a wonderful sunny day with five knots of easterly and as we fished out from Stevensons Island where we'd anchored overnight we got a bite on the long rigger.

There being nothing to see other than the odd swirl and a rap on the lure. A small "stick" appeared and rapped the lure, there was an odd swirl and the line ran out.

We were hooked-up.

"What the Hell was that?" asked Captain John, "I can see the lure in the water but not the fish."

A few minutes later the culprit was exposed, it's brilliant colours shining for all to see.

Another spearfish, again about 15 kilos, a totally lit up, feisty little devil. With it's long dorsal right along it's back it seemed to be able to swim backwards like an eel or a catfish and I was amazed that it had the nerve to attack a big lure with such determination.

A couple of hours later we had a repeat performance on the shotgun- the spearfish expert was at it again. Like London buses, I had waited a lifetime then three spearfish had showed up one after the other.

"I could get used to this on 10 kilo gear."

We turned around and fished back up the coast. As we crossed Doubtless Bay, a school of sauries burst clear of the surface closely followed by a marauding marlin and we worked around the area and along a mucky current line.

The rigger popped.

Like before I reeled in.

"I can see the lure but not the fish, must be another spearfish," informed the skipper.

But this was no spearfish, even though it fought like a spearfish.

It was a clear plastic bag with a live crab in it.

So now you know, spearfish fight like plastic bags, on 37kg anyway.

With all the other game-boats concentrated between Cape Brett and Tutukaka, we were on our own again as we went into Cape Karikari for the night and I felt a lot jollier than I had done for a while.

Of course it was not to last.

The water was still green and looked that way all the way to North Cape so the next day we headed back the way we had come. We were barely in 120 metres and still in the green water when a striped marlin launched itself into our spread and ran off with a lure.

The line disappeared from the reel in a very satisfactory manner. At last, this looked like the business.

The Captain must have thought so because in the ensuing excitement, he was making a call on the radio to report the hook-up but before I could say "Not yet!" the deed was done and before long replies of "Don't lose it!" and "Make sure you get it to the boat!" were being made on channel 62 by the Whangaroa Club faithful; keen to claim the season's first marlin.

Of course, at this point the marlin decided to put in an appearance and after three or four hounding jumps and thrashing headshakes, it threw the hook.

Unlike the sea, the air was blue and I felt like a leper.

"Well I know one thing we won't do when we next get hooked up." I said miserably.

"Yup, so do I," agreed the Captain.

Unable to mask our disappointment we headed out to deeper water as if to run away from the scene of our embarrassment.

The sea became flat and oily, the wind dropped to nothing and you could see the surface clear to the horizon in all directions. The water temperature began to shoot up and we entered a stretch of water that was over 23°C and a tropical indigo blue as though we had been transported to another place.

Zoë had sucked the water behind it on its run down from the tropics and areas that were three and a half degrees less a few hours earlier were now up to 23.7°C.

"Mind that big log over there John, it's over ten feet long," I advised the Captain.

"What log?"

"Over to the starboard, by that sunfish."

"Eh? I can see the sunfish."

I stood up to point out the tree trunk I had observed wallowing on the surface.

It wasn't there. But I too could see the sunfish.

"But it was right there, it couldn't just disappear."

I scanned around and low and behold the log popped up right beside the boat no more than thirty feet away.

"Bloody Hell! It's a BROADBILL!"

All eyes diverted to the spot and sure enough there it was – a big broadbill probably 250 kilos and just cruising quietly along on the surface.

"Get a bait, get a squid, quick!" Captain John was leaping about like a headless chicken.

Within minutes there was a couple of still-frozen squid in the water.

"What do we do now?"

"Zane Grey! Where are you when we need you?"

In 1923 Zane Grey, sight-fishing for broadbill off Catalina Island, California, sighted 140 fish, baited 94, had 11 strikes, hooked 7 and landed 4.

I know how he must have felt.

"A shortbilled spearfish! The first one I'd caught, in fact the first live one I'd ever seen."

Like Zane Grey, we quietly towed the squid around trying to get one in front of the disinterested swordfish. We must have followed for over a mile before the fish went down.

Like Zane Grey, I held my breath waiting for the strike but the only thing that appeared behind the squid was a manta ray. It swam right up and inspected the bait very carefully. The bait was pulled away and the manta ray followed. Again the squid was led away and the ray swam right up to it again. It was fascinating to watch and something that was to occur again more spectacularly later in the trip.

"OK — that's enough, get the lures back out," came the instructions from above.

We followed the wonderful water down past the Cavallis and caught another plastic bag (sans crab).

No a real plastic bag, a red one, not a spearfish impersonating a plastic bag.

Past the Cavallis and towards the Nine Pin a vast area was alive with sauries. The dolphins and gannets were going crazy. A gannet dived on top of a dolphin as it surfaced and nearly knocked itself out, it sat shaking it's head and another dolphin crashed by sending it zooming back up into the sky. It was bizarre.

"Another spearfish, again about 15 kilos, a totally lit up, feisty little devil."

There just had to be marlin here somewhere.

We worked back around and the long rigger was knocked out closely followed by the long corner. There was nothing to see.

Maybe our buddies again.

Back past the Cavallis and the same happened to the short rigger and the short corner. Still nothing to see, still no hook-up.

Then the long rigger popped and the line ran out — a hook-up, at last!

"What is it, I can see the lure but not the fish."

It sounded a touch familiar.

That's because it was another plastic bag — a blue one.

"We're on bloody litter duty," said the smirking deckhand, disgustedly.

It was an eventful day but with nothing to show for it but a bagful of rubbish and as I knew it would, Zoë decided to come back.

For four days it rained and rained and we towed lures, relentlessly up and down, over the same area until my attention chip melted.

I'd had enough.

We were wet, we were hot and it was humid and sticky.

Tempers began to fray.

"Bloody Wurzels!"

Looking for excuses for our failure, Mike's "scarecrows" were unfairly coming in for some stick.

We ran in early to the Cavallis and the rain stopped.

As we entered Takou Bay and before the anchor went down, Mike jumped out of the marlin door for a dip and a cool down.

The skipper idled one engine and Mike disappeared, sucked down by the prop wash only to pop up again, spluttering and gasping for breath.

"Did you see that?" asked the skipper.

"No, see what?"

So he did it again.

This time Mike span around before disappearing and came back up, bum first, drinking his fill.

"Cor! Better not try both engines, eh?"

The next night Mike took a dip in the bait tank instead but he got out before we could get the lid down.

It was time for an executive decision.

Tomorrow we would do something different.

To some muttering from above we caught kahawai and towed livebaits around the Taheke Reef until the plotter was just a big black blob and the kahawai gave up the ghost.

Undaunted, I then got the boys to rig a skip bait and a swim bait, a la Cairns, and we didn't even get a bite from a shark.

After a few hours I could sense the captain had had enough so I relented and the lures went back out and we slipped uncomfortably back into the lone furrow we had ploughed for days and days and headed up the coast again.

We hadn't gone far when a marlin tailed down the port side and gave the lure on the shotgun a whack before disappearing.

At least it had stopped raining.

Everything else was the same.

Eventually Zoë got pushed out to the east of New Zealand and a high began building. The forecast looked good for the foreseeable future so it was goodbye to the coast and back off into the wide blue yonder.

It was a straight run north, out to the 60 Mile Ground and the Cavalli seamount. Maybe this time there would be something at home.

Unlike before Christmas the albacore were absent and all was quiet.

That night the abominable squid was ceremoniously lowered, with little hope and some desperation to an imaginary 21 gun salute and all was peaceful until at 6am, just before daybreak, we got the Shimano wake up call.

I fell out of my bunk and crashed into a deckhand, stubbing his big toe and causing it to spurt claret everywhere and with the skipper close behind we burst onto the deck like the Keystone Cops.

I pushed up the drag and wound the line tight.

"Yup, we're on."

Buckled in the chair, I got to work.

The fish was on the surface and showing all the signs of being a small shark.

By now, anything would do. We must have drifted a squid for more than ten nights without a touch. At least this fish had had the common decency to wait until we were just about to get up anyway.

I worked the fish towards the boat with minimum resistance and thinking, "It's a shark" I was using little finesse and giving the fish no time to get its head.

Imagine my surprise when the skipper cried out incredulously.

"It's a sword! It's a bloody swordie!"

Back in the early days of broadbill fishing in the 1910s and 20s nobody would purposefully fish at night for broadbill. Although some battles went into and through the night, some of the most famous anglers of the time would break off rather than go into darkness attached to the "Gladiator."

They wouldn't have worried about this sucker! It was the most perfect little broadbill you could ever wish to see, all of 40 kilos with the sharpest of swords, as the claret-spouting deckhand soon found out.

I had always wanted to tag and release a broadbill and my wish was fulfilled.

It was a lovely moment and we were all thrilled by such a surprise.

I had now caught broadbill in three different places in New Zealand, here at the Cavalli seamount, the King Bank and the Western Ground by the Middlesex Bank. I had tagged four billfish so far for the new season and incredibly not one of them a marlin!

On a bit of a high we towed lures again all day but I was beginning to resign myself to the likelihood that I would have to wait a bit longer for

"some of the most famous anglers of the time would break off rather than go into darkness attached to the "Gladiator.""

"It was the most perfect little broadbill you could ever wish to see, all of 40 kilos with the sharpest of swords, as the claret-spouting deckhand soon found out."

the "big blue". Unlike the previous January when they had turned up in good numbers not one blue marlin had been reported anywhere as yet. So I agreed with the captain that we should forget it and go back to where we had a better chance of breaking the ice with a striped marlin.

The following day we fished back to the Garden Patch and searched the canyons one last time before heading back towards Cape Karikari and the Doubtless Bay area where most of our marlin sightings had been made.

Other than Captain John, we had all eaten our dinners when someone else was sent up to take the helm whilst he came down into the saloon for his. After a few mouthfuls, the boat altered course noticeably.

"I hope he's got a good reason for changing course, I was heading to where we got a bite before," growled the skipper, hunched over his lamb chops.

The scream from the bridge closely followed by the scream from the reel provided the answer. The new helmsman had seen a large aluminium can glinting in the lowering sun and had gone to investigate. A marlin, which must have been driven crazy by the shining, bobbing and flashing can, shot out and ate the first lure it saw.

We were in business!

Conscious of our two other failures I was sitting on eggs in the chair and played the fish as carefully and calmly as my thumping heart would allow.

The fish jumped but didn't jump off. It dug in but didn't pull the hook. It ran off again but surrendered quietly. In fact it was perfectly well behaved, came to the boat without too much fuss, accepted the tag, lay quietly while the hook was removed, lit up it's stripes like a zebra and swam off strongly to the great relief of us all.

It was short and fat and was called 95 kilos although to me at least it looked bigger.

After 23 days at sea and thousands of miles of trolling lures we finally had tagged a marlin in sight of the bloody harbour! It wasn't the blue I was after, that had to wait until the next trip, when all that had passed, all the paying of dues, all the frustration and anguish, all the tedium and boredom, all the trial and error would be swept away forever in a veritable "marlin-fest" on the King Bank.

Amazingly the "Zebra" was recaptured a few weeks later by another boat fishing outside the Manakau Harbour on the west coast, the fish having travelled back up around the top of New Zealand and down the other coast. Its captors called it 115 kilos and I am pleased to say they retagged and released it.

There was one day left, the last of our 17 day mission and with it one more surprise and one of the most unusual battles I have ever enjoyed.

We were outside Stevensons Island in the company of one or two other boats one of which was reporting marlin sightings. We could plainly see the "tailing marlin" to be manta rays. We had two mackerel livebaits out and the other boat was trolling round and zooming from one leaping manta ray to the next. The radio was full of chatter and more boats appeared on the horizon, heading our way.

This in itself was amusing enough and the mirthful cries of derision poured forth unabatedly from our decks.

One of our livebaits began to get nervous and swam up to the surface closely attended by a manta ray. Another manta ray appeared, then another, until there were seven mobbing the panic stricken mackerel.

It was obvious what would happen next as one of the manta rays swam down the line and got hooked in its wing.

I have never seen line leave a reel so fast. The spool became so hot I could not put a hand on the reel, only the handle. We had no choice but to chase off after the rapidly disappearing Dacron backing, backing up at such speed, for all intents and purposes to our onlookers, hooked-up to a marlin. Our action intensifying, if it were possible, the frantic activities of the other gameboats around us.

As we quickly left the scene I pushed the drag up towards the maximum, which only served to plane the manta ray up to the surface, and it began to jump, spectacularly flapping its wings like a gigantic bird.

After ten minutes or so we began to make ground and fight the fish to the boat. It's immense power made me strain every sinew to control the recovery of the line and it was a great relief to me when the leader appeared and I was able to hand the fish over to the leaderman who wasn't quite sure what to expect.

Clinging on grimly and setting his feet, he gritted his teeth and heaved.

The hook pulled, the fish burst out and we watched it jumping and jumping, like a skimming pebble, off and endlessly away towards Cape Brett.

Exhilarated but slightly embarrassed we crept away leaving the rest of the fleet hunting more "marlin".

I was surprised when Captain John announced on the radio that we'd only hooked a manta ray.

The rest of us could gleefully have had a lot more fun at the other boats' expense but you might be interested to learn that even though he can get a bit grumpy when a fish gets off, it doesn't mean to say that the skipper's not a nice kind chap really.

The Mission

Part 3 – "Mission Accomplished"

In life you don't expect to get something for nothing, some may do but find that it was only a loan and one way or another they pay eventually, but twenty four days at sea and more dollars spent than I care to admit to, for one striped marlin, left me thinking that payday was not too far away.

That's not to say it would just be "a gimme", the homework had continued, details from all the likely spots had been collected and the weather and SST charts had been studied relentlessly. The west coast was beginning to show some fish and there was plenty of bait round there, fuel and stores were organised should we decide to make the long run to Reef Point and maybe down past Baylys Beach to Glinks Gully.

The prospect of fishing the east coast again was depressing even though patches of fish had shown up, also it was the week of the Whangaroa One Base, a tournament we were expected to enter and defend. But a couple of days before we were due to sail, I got the call I was hoping for.

That day two boats had each tagged two marlin on the King Bank.

Once relayed to John Gregory, the skipper of *Primetime*, that was it. We were off, and off in the morning!

Almost a year earlier *Primetime* had gone to the Three Kings in the NZ Nationals and caught twenty-eight striped marlin, fifteen more than their nearest competitor and all on lures. There had been three anglers on board and one had caught ten fish. I wanted to do that. I normally fish alone maybe I could get the whole 28!

I was particularly excited when we left the next morning, I had a good feeling, if the other boats could get two a day, we could get three or four. The weather forecast looked great and there was a couple of spare days at the end of my charter if we could get the fuel to last.

Oh boy! I couldn't wait to get there!

Outside Stevensons Island we saw two tailing marlin side-by-side in about 120 metres.

A few miles further on we saw another but we couldn't hang around, we were on a mission.

Off Doubtless Bay we caught one of our "usuals".

A "plastic bag", the fishy type.

Our fourth shortbilled spearfish of the season, this one a bit bigger at eighteen kilos.

A good start but we didn't delay; we were being drawn inexorably north.

We towed lures past North Cape and got in touch with the boats on the King Bank.

Pack attacks, doubles, trebles; they'd had a busy day but not got too many to stick, although one boat had tagged three striped marlin and a mako.

We planned to run through to the Three Kings, get blue koheru in the morning for livebaits and then attack the King Bank. The bait rods were set up and the tuna berley was mashed up in the bucket.

But it was all put away again.

There was a better idea.

Run straight to the King Bank, drift around for a bit, then be right on the spot at daybreak and catch a couple before the other boats arrived.

I love it! What a great plan and boy, did it pay off?

At four in the morning we were drifting a squid outside the King Bank and at six o'clock I caught a 150 kilo mako after a savage five-minute slugging match that saw the fish at the boat green and unhappy.

Most sharks, makos especially, have really tough skin, getting a tag in can sometimes not be the easiest of jobs and only serves to really stir up an already agitated and uncooperative fish. This mako was a bit of a pig.

Mike was struggling to hold it on the leader and the first crack with the long tag pole only managed to bend the tag over. The skipper, conscious of his brand new gel-coat and the mass of gnashing teeth, sensibly ordered the fish to be cut off.

It was a good warm-up, the lures were put out and we got to work. Work which, in the daylight hours anyway, was to continue almost non-stop for seven days and produce the most amazing striped marlin fishing you could ever wish to experience anywhere in the world.

Fishing like it must have been in Grey's time, imagine if he had made it to the Kings!

At seven o'clock I caught the first striped marlin of about 90 kilos.

It didn't mess about, it just came straight in, dorsal erect and quivering, and ate the lure.

By the time the other boats had come out from North West Bay and run the twenty miles to the top of the King Bank, I had hooked two more, both of which had jumped off after a few minutes.

"The captain had promised beer for the lads if we got to twenty"

It was quiet until at just after one o'clock there was another, no-nonsense bite and I tagged another stripey of 80 kilos. As the lures were being run out we were bit again with the same result, this time a fish of 100 kilos. Both fish fought the same. After an aggressive bite and hook-up, they crashed around, jumped a bit before settling down for us to go over and collect.

So far, so good, three tagged out of five, all on lures and only one other fish between the other boats. We were the business!

The last fish had chafed up the leader and the lure needed to be re-rigged, so while Matt did the necessary, Mike took the opportunity to run out one of his Wurzels.

We didn't get another bite.

"The bait has gone down," he insisted.

"Oh, yeah?"

"You wait and see, you mock all you like. You'll be choking!"

"I already am."

We left the Bank reasonably early to get back to North West Bay, put out the cray pot and try and get some koheru, which we didn't get. There was a strong tide running and even though we could see them on the sounder they wouldn't come up.

"Don't worry John, we got marlin easily enough today on lures, let's hope for the best."

I tried to placate the skipper.

"Yeah, that's fine but we will need to conserve fuel at some point if we are going to stay out here for a week."

The next morning at first light, with a crayfish safely in the bait tank we set off again for our "hot-spot". About three quarters of the way in no-man's land we got a double hook-up. I played mine from the chair and Matt fought his stand-up. Luckily mine went deep and kept out of the way but Matt's eventually jumped off after an aerial battle. I struggled with mine for twenty minutes to try and get it to come up and when I felt the telltale bouncing of the rod, as it got closer, I feared the worst. The fish had been wrapped up, was getting unwrapped and would soon be gone.

As we got to the top of the Bank I hooked-up twice in quick succession. The first came out straight away and jumped off and the second just sat there "window-wiping" and threw the hook. What a start! It was barely eight thirty and we'd already lost four fish.

I checked for Wurzels but they were still safely waiting on the rigging bench.

At midday we were pack-attacked.

Properly pack-attacked. Not where a couple of fish come in and whack out all the lures but where all the lures get eaten at once, there are fins scything all over the place, each time a lure is dropped another fish grabs it and when all four reels are haemorrhaging line there are still marlin pouring in trying to find something to eat, even a Wurzel.

Concentrating on my fish I didn't see Mike lose what was a really big fish after a while, another having dropped off before the skipper could leave the helm. So that left Matt and I.

Matt had been helped into the stand-up harness and I got to work as we tried to keep our fish apart. I got mine of about 80 kilos in twenty minutes in which time the other had taken its chance to get a long way away and not be very cooperative. With Matt's cries of "FISH ON!" and trying to waggle his bum and tits like Tara, it was another half an hour before it was finally tagged. As all the lures, hooks and leaders needed checking it was the reserve team that was run out, including a Wurzel and a big lumo softhead on the long rigger that got whacked immediately.

The fish didn't hook-up but it came back and grabbed it again, ran off twenty metres before dropping it, turning and grabbing it again and then finally on the fourth attempt it found the hook and went crazy. Boy it was mad! It jumped itself to a standstill to an admiring audience and we followed before creeping over and tagging it, another of 100 kilos.

No sooner than the lures were out again, we got a shot on the long corner, a shot on the short rigger and a couple of lookers.

Things were slowing up a bit!

From one thirty to just before five o'clock we got some welcome respite and a chance to get all the gear presentable again, hooks sharpened and re-taped, leaders replaced, drags checked, but at five o'clock the fish got hungry again and came back with a vengeance.

It was non-stop.

Shots, hook-ups, doubles, chaos but it wasn't until six thirty that I got one to stick and another 100 kilo striped marlin was duly tagged. Again, three for the day for me.

The action continued for thirty minutes and included a spearfish the captain could plainly see from up top before it got off, until at seven o'clock a huge fish crashed a lure. I grabbed the rod but I felt it get off just as it crashed another lure, which Mike struck successfully. The fish, feeling the hook, spun round in a surge of white water and took off, taking my line with it.

"We're on a double!" shouted the captain.

"No I don't think so," I said, "I reckon we're both on the same fish, a bloody big mako!"

The mako had grabbed my lure, opened its mouth to eat the second, dropping the first in the process and as it turned back to make its escape, got my hook in its tail.

What a mess!

We couldn't unravel the line, as every time the fish changed direction it would twist the line up even more. Of course we didn't know any of this at the time and with Mike on stand-up and me in the chair we were grunting and groaning trying to subdue the monster, which was not very happy.

Mike was not only getting some "noise" from the bridge, he also got some over the radio from the skipper of another boat he used to work on.

"Tell him he's on 37 kilo now, not four. Put your back into it you lazy slob!"

But no matter what we did, even with two sets of 37 kilo gear at full sunset, with the shark shackled in a cats cradle, we were struggling. I would try maximum pressure from the chair and Mike would take a rest, but I'd be pulling on the tail and getting nowhere. Mike would take over and if I eased up we would make some ground until Mike would take a rest. I could feel the line grating on the other and was surprised it didn't snap under so much pressure. All the time the bridge was bleating about "lost bite time on a lousy shark" and Mike and I would look at each other and shrug. It was hard going but we had some fun with that fish but nothing like the fun when after nearly an hour we got a very unhappy shark of 300 kilos right to the boat.

The real fun now began as the task of retrieving all the gear, especially the lures, swivels and wind on leaders, lay in store.

The shark was recovering and wavering around from one side of the boat to the other with Matt holding on bravely but the sight of 6 feet 5inch John Gregory steaming fearlessly into the fray to get back his expensive equipment was enough for the shark to settle enough to be tagged, untangled, cursed and finally released for the loss of one hook.

The Mission — Part 3 – "Mission Accomplished"

It was after eight o'clock but there was time for another bite before we shut down for a broadbill drift and for the two rods used on the mako to be top-shotted and all the leaders to be checked and repaired

Day three on the King Bank, after an undisturbed night, saw the lures out at first light but we saw nothing until at ten past four in the afternoon a big blue marlin appeared out of nowhere and monstered the long rigger, it missed the lure, turned back, tried again and only succeeded in getting wrapped up in the leader.

I settled into the fight but when the fish didn't jump and didn't rush about I knew it wasn't feeling the hook and that my chances were slim. Like Don King said about Frank Bruno when he was to defend his World Heavyweight title against Mike Tyson, "Bruno's got two chances against Tyson, None and Slim, and Slim has just left town!"

The blue marlin just sulked, leaving it to me to make things happen and it came as no surprise, although seriously disappointing, when, with me increasing the pressure to make some progress, the fish unwrapped

---

"It was a good fish, at least 140 kilos and I was stuffed."

and was gone.

I was cross. A big blue marlin and it was gone. I sulked and fell into a sullen silence.

"Don't worry John, we're in the old "ten-past" groove, that fish bit at ten past four, you wait until ten past five!" Matt reminded me of one of our reliable superstitions.

With the occasional growl or two I sunk a couple of bottles of best German brew and as I mellowed out in my lucky fishing seat I watched a big striped marlin dorsal, lit up neon blue, zigzag in behind the short corner, line up with a quiver and, Bang!

It was eight minutes past five.

The fish took off leaping and leaping, shooting around three parts of a circle, forcing us to take off before it jumped back over the line. This fish was hot, it didn't stop but with me cranking like crazy we were hot on its tail and had the tag in the same time as grabbing the leader. It had taken most of the day but we had caught another fish of around 100 kilos. Straightaway I lost another that just sat there window wiping and was off before we could get back onto it.

"Dinner is on the table," called Mike.

"What's the time? Six-fifteen, should be safe now." So we all went in and sat down.

I picked up my knife and fork, (we have proper meals you know, not sloshed in a bowl and served with a spoon) and a reel went off. I rushed out to see a striped marlin going ballistic, doing cartwheels and backwards somersaults like a mako. Another hot fish of about 120 kilos, they were getting bigger, was quickly subdued and we took off back to North West Bay to get another "bug" out of the cray pot and prepare for an early start on the blue koheru in the morning.

You don't get to see John Gregory fishing very much, occasionally snapper fishing but always when it's time to catch koheru for livebaits. Watching him it is easy to see the burning passion inside as he moves up a couple of gears and goes at it with a matchless intensity. I'd love to see him on a marlin or better still a big mako or even a broadbill but I doubt it will happen unless we are on some other person's boat.

"I'm not letting any other joker drive my boat, certainly not if we have a fish on!" he was horrified at the thought of it.

"Maybe if we run the shotgun from the bridge?" I suggested lamely.

The skipper having done his fishing for the trip and filled the bait tank, it was time to return to the King Bank.

Nine marlin so far in three days but the big man wasn't happy.

"More doubles and trebles is what we need."

I was happy with one at a time, thankyou very much but when did it matter what the customer thought?

It was a quiet morning with only a couple of half-hearted shots and enquiries so about eleven thirty we put out the livebaits.

The first one slipped its bridle and another broke its docking ring. Two more went out and before the third went over one of the others got mako'd. The shark took off over the surface like a marlin before being bullied back and tagged. Over the next three hours it was mako mayhem as I caught another two and lost three more that bit through the mono.

The three we got to the boat were all 120–130 kilos and gave the usual virtuoso mako leaps, cartwheels and somersaults.

The only other incident resulted in the two lads being summoned to the bridge for a verbal ear bashing of epic proportions.

Two livebaits were out and Mike was lowering a third over when it shot under the boat and the leader got caught up on something on the port side.

Whoops.

The captain came down. Words were spoken.

Matt volunteered to dive in and free the line.

"I'll go," said Mike to nobody in particular.

Matt stripped off and was about to go over when the skipper said,

"Hold on, I'll move the boat away from the bait school."

Matt, who up to then seemed keen to jump in, suddenly was less enamoured with the idea and it took a couple of prods with the tag pole to see him fulfil his duty like a man.

As he went down a stream of bubbles rose from his boxers, I had to look away.

He was barely wet before he was back on deck with the leader, which had been wrapped around the zinc on the end of the propeller.

"Nice of the boss to move away from the sharks before I went over."

"Yeah, I don't think he'd have done it for Mike."

So it was back to the lures and whilst Mike muttered to himself about his Wurzels still being dry and threatening to unrig them, I hooked-up on a nice marlin of 100 kilos, the first of the day. It was followed on the score sheet at ten past four by another of 110 kilos, one which didn't jump and I thought might be wrapped. So we took it softly, softly until we got the tag in and it could be leadered more aggressively.

At a quarter to seven I got a third that jumped all the way back to the boat, swam under and recommenced jumping again on the other side, all of which caused some panic on the deck and some frantic evasive action before we caught up with it and got the tag in.

A fourth fish, a nice one of 120 kilos, piled on late at eight o'clock and jumped continuously until we got it grudgingly under control and seen to.

Another good day, our fourth on the King Bank, we'd gone four for four on marlin in the afternoon and evening but the best was yet to come. After a very shaky start, tomorrow was to be a belter!

That night we moved a few miles uptide so that we would drift back to our hot spot again first thing in the morning.

At seven in the morning, fifteen minutes after the lures had got wet, we got pack attacked.

We had four on, the captain crashing down the stairs was enough to make the unaccounted for one drop off and Matt's one departed after a while too which left, after about ten minutes, just Mike and myself to do battle. The fish disappeared in opposite directions and for once I let mine run, to get Mike's first. I made a mistake.

Mike didn't have a harness on at first and was using his testicles as a 37kg bent-butt rod gimbal. I found his repeated whimpering very disconcerting and told him so – from the comfort of my fighting chair. With all the mono long gone and the Dacron backing disappearing from my reel I tried to encourage Mike.

"Get cranking you fat prawn! Stop whining and get winding! Why are you standing there like you've crapped yourself?"

This was mild compared to the judgement from King Solomon raining down from on high.

Matt helped him into the stand-up harness and Mike was able to breathe out for the first time in ten minutes, the blood returning to his loins made his eyes water as he began the pitiful task of line recovery.

"Just close your eyes and think of Carmen, the pain will go away."

"Thanks John, you're a great help," Mike wobbled about, collecting line and doing his best.

"Those belts are designed for someone with a waist, I don't think it should be where it is, you know."

"Get off my back, will you!"

"If I got on your back it might help you stand up straight."

By the time Mike was back on the mono, I was down to a fifty cent piece and aware that I had half a mile of line to rewind.

Shoot, this ain't good, Johnnie-boy, no good at all!

Matt collected the leader on Mike's fish and mine got bored and began to jump, looking like a saury in the distance and I felt sick as I imagined it had come unstuck. So I wound.

I wound for ages and ages and the skipper eased the boat backwards and an uneasy silence fell over the boat. I wound and I wound and I got hot and tired and my uneasy silence turned into a mounting disquiet. I wound every last centimetre of line back on the reel until the lure hit the back of the boat. I threw off the buckles from the harness, plunged the rod in the holder, drew myself up and marched up the stairs.

Not nice words were spoken and I marched down again.

It would be hours before I spoke any more. I needed time to stew and get over it.

Nice singles, that's all I wanted, doubles and trebles spelled disaster, and I could only reel one in at a time.

The spell had broken, I could feel it, for the time being my luck had run out, I knew what to do, so I took it on the chin and moved on.

It was only minutes before we got hit again, I grabbed the rod on the short corner, and the fish quickly ran out 100 metres and jumped off. Another fish hit the short rigger, as I turned to grab the rod, Matt was standing there holding it up so I could get to the chair with the short corner that had just got off.

"Oh, for ***ks sake!" I yelled.

"It's OK, Its OK! I haven't touched the drag. It's not struck," pleaded Matt, frozen to the spot.

Unconvinced I took the rod from him, got in the chair and played the fish for a few minutes before it fell off. I slowly reeled all the line back before returning to my lucky fishing seat, which was no longer on fire.

The spell had definitely broken.

"John, would you come up to the bridge please, I'd like to have a word with you," demanded the captain, very headmaster-like.

"Not just now I'll talk to you later."

It would not have been pretty; some things are best left alone.

But it wasn't over yet.

The next fish jumped off before I could get in the harness.

The uneasy silence got uneasier.

Another chance, the next fish smashed the lure like a blue marlin and crashed about like one before I got it to the boat and we tagged a stripey of about 120 kilos.

It was my fourteenth of the season but now I was on thirteen for the trip.

Any idea that things had improved was quickly dispelled when the next fish grabbed the lure rushed up the port side and jumped off in front of the boat.

The next fish I fought all the way to the boat and after twenty minutes, just as the leader was going to be collected, the hook pulled out.

It wasn't yet midday, I'd caught one out of six and I wasn't talking to anybody.

Bloody thirteens.

I lay down on the deck and went to sleep – perhaps I'll wake up and it would have been a bad dream.

I woke up just after one o'clock feeling better and the bad dream ended.

For the rest of the day, right up until dark at nine o'clock, it was total carnage and at the end of it I would no longer be on thirteen but on eighteen for the trip and the boat on twenty-one!

I was grabbing a drink of water and stretching the sleep and ache out of my bones when a blue marlin hurtled through the spread chasing a bunch of mahimahi. A reel screamed but it was a foul-hooked mahimahi that came to the boat. We stayed with the school of mahimahi with everyone totally focussed and expectant. At times the mahimahi were massed around the lures, maybe that was the reason we were pack attacked again.

With three marlin firmly hooked the skipper struggled to get the fourth lure in without it getting eaten, although it was chased right back to the transom by a fish lit up like a Christmas tree with its pectorals splayed out like a big bird. It swerved away just before the moment of impact, I could have tagged it from the chair on its way by.

When the dust settled Matt, myself and Mike were spread across the stern, all harnessed up, rods arced over and leaning into three striped marlin, all in the air together, 150–200 metres behind us. We could see that Mike's was a really big fish. It was pandemonium for a while as Matt and Mike switched sides continually and we took lines under or over until we were, all three of us directly connected to our respective fish which, on settling down, had gone in different directions.

Not making the mistake of earlier in the day I got to work straight away, Matt had to work his way up to the bow and Mike's big fish just kept going down swell away to the port-side. It was nearly thirty minutes before the first fish got off. It was hapless Mike's and he started muttering darkly. He had a mile of line to recover and we couldn't move until he'd got it all back on. I got mine of around 90 kilos to the boat and we were able to get Matt back from the bow and go after his. He declined the use of the chair and tiredly worked the stand-up to a successful conclusion as Mike grabbed the leader and I was ready to stick it with the tag.

"There's your shot," Matt yelled.

"I can't even see the fish."

"Just follow the line down and take your best shot."

"No wonder your tag placings are a bit erratic," I replied remembering the fish with the tag closer to the anal fin than the dorsal, "No I'm not going to stick its eye or gill, you bring the fish up a bit I'm not sure my luck has returned yet."

A couple of winds and there it was and I put the tag right on the spot, perfect.

"You wouldn't be happy if I had waited like that," said Matt.

"Yeah, but it wasn't my fish."

I knew things were back to the way they should be when we got two doubles in quick succession thereafter and it was my two of 100 and 110 kilos that stayed stuck. Mike who had just seen yet another really big one jump off was muttering even more.

"Yours was a big sucker Mike."

"Bloody thirteen, I hate it."

"Forget it Mike I've got sixteen now."

"Not you, you plonker, me! I am stuck on thirteen marlin."

"Oh, shoot! Don't worry we'll get you one, I'll put you in the chair as soon as I can."

"No, I'm not touching another rod, I am a curse. I'm not going to be the one who prevents us breaking the record."

"What record, what are you on about?"

"Twenty-eight, that's the boat's best tally for one trip."

"Oh blimey, no wonder he wants doubles and trebles."

"Nothing like a bit of pressure, eh?"

"Not a good time to suggest putting out a Wurzel or two then?"

"John! Will you stop it please, you're getting me down."

"Leave it to me, one way or another, you're going to get a fish and we're going to get more than twenty-eight."

So I wasn't the only one on a mission.

Bloody hell what have I gone and promised now?

The Fatal Greek Sister Lachesis who destined my appointed lot and spun the thread of my life wasn't about to let me down now — all would be well!

The next fish was a real stubborn so-and-so, it just would not give up, the leader was collected three or four times and it still powered away.

"Don't grab it next time, I'll wind up as much as I can and you stick it with the tag."

"All right, I'll just crook the leader over my hand."

The newly introduced twelve foot tag-pole had really earned its stripes on this trip, even if some of the placements were a bit off. As soon as the fish felt the tag go in it was off again but it meant Mike could really lean into the fish when I brought it up for the last time. It was a good fish, at least 140 kilos and I was stuffed.

I ran my head under the tap as the lures went out again and before I had recovered my breath we were bit again.

I had to take my time, I had no choice, and my right shoulder would barely rotate.

"Blimey, I've done some work today."

Things were beginning to catch up with me as I got the 120 kilo fish to the boat.

I was five-for-five since the morning's debacle, which was all but forgotten and we were eight-for-eighteen for the day. Eighteen hooked fish! What a day!

But you know what?

Tomorrow would be even better.

Especially when the Wurzel went out.

The captain had promised beer for the lads if we got to twenty and cans and bottles had mysteriously appeared from secret places and the cooler was stacked, he even had three himself, until the Stella ran out and it was down to that miserable NZ brew that someone called Bill likes!

We stayed put again that night, it was an easy way to save fuel and give us the maximum time in the strike zone. All the other boats always ran back to the Islands and missed the early and late bites every day. I couldn't understand it, it was flat calm most nights and we would hear them complaining about their anchorages on the radio and just shake our heads. They would joke about **Primetime** forgetting how to put the anchor down and "stretching the line every night" but we caught more fish while they were travelling backwards and forwards than they all caught collectively in the whole week.

I doubt that we had moved more than a couple of miles in any direction while fishing and there was one particular hot spot that we coveted. Lots of information had been relayed over the radio to deter too much close attention but even when other boats strayed closer it was us that hooked-up and I could imagine the grinding of teeth taking place at other helms. It would have been audible if they had known the truth.

I caught eight fish on this our sixth day on the King Bank, not all striped marlin but with an average size of nearly 160 kilos plus another few that I played right to the boat before disaster set in, I was physically knackered at the end. During the day the brain was issuing alarm signals

---

"monstrous 160 kilo plus striped marlin, all lit up, stripes a blazing, dorsal erect but looking slightly embarrassed with a bright yellow tag stuck on top of its head."

about the punishment the ageing frame had to bear but as always the adrenalin did its job and I survived to fight another day.

The day began as others had, at around seven thirty we had a double on. I urged a reluctant Mike to take the other, a really big one, but they both fell off after a protracted struggle.

At eight thirtyish a big mako came out and smashed the lure, beating the water to foam as it felt the hook. Not wanting to waste time I went to the maximum and bullied and harried the bemused shark, all of 180 kilos, into Mike's waiting hands and the tag was punched home.

The next fish, at ten o'clock was a big striped marlin, we knew when it jumped that it was a bit special and I was over tentative, as I didn't want to lose it. I stayed off the drag, allowed it to settle and stay up on top and we crept over and tried to collect it. It was cruising along nicely as Mike gently pinched the leader and Matt stood like a heron waiting to pounce with the long tag pole.

"Whoa, steady on," cried Mike as the marlin began to wake up.

"Oo'er," said Matt as he stood back with the tag pole missing its tag.

"I couldn't help it, it just turned round and swam into it."

The skipper came down, I jumped out of the chair and we looked over to see a monstrous 160 kilo plus striped marlin, all lit up, stripes a blazing, dorsal erect but looking slightly embarrassed with a bright yellow tag stuck on top of its head.

"Never mind, let's get another one," urged the captain, lifting the marlin up by its bill until its eye was level with the belting. Matt slipped the hook out and the big man shot the marlin off like a javelin.

"Come on lets get another double!" and he ran up the stairs back to his post as the rest of us looked at each other, for once speechless.

At eleven o'clock or thereabouts another big mako found a taste for plastic and a fast and furious battle ensued as it somersaulted back towards the boat.

"Let's see the old bugger lift this one up!" I cheerfully called to the lads who suddenly weren't there anymore.

The shark was leaping clear up into the sky every twenty metres or so, the next jump should be about forty metres away, Ah yes, there it goes. That means...

That means, it's brown trouser time!

I couldn't go anywhere. For all intents and purposes I was strapped in.

The next leap was right on cue.

The "old bugger" must have heard me, the boat never moved.

Well that's it then. Nobody would ever read about what happened on the King Bank in February 2003. It was all for nothing, I was history, brother.

What a way to go, I never did get that big blue.

Goodbye world.

My temporary dementia was interrupted by the line coming up tight, the rod pulling down and the chair wrenching round to my left, as the mako missed its chance to taste more than plastic, shot under the boat and recommenced its somersaults out on the starboard side.

"Sucker!" I screamed, ever so bravely and we were off and after it and a 200 kilo mako was tagged and cut away.

I was pumped all right but needed a trip to the head to rearrange my underwear.

As I vacated the premises the captain came down to utilise the same service. He seemed inordinately jolly. The rotten bastard.

"Don't get a triple," he jokingly instructed Mike who was sent to take over upstairs.

Shorts were down, around the ankles probably, and we got mobbed.

It started as a treble but when a giant sunfish was flushed from the head one quickly dropped off (or expired) and it was left to Matt and I. Mine threw the hook after a while and I got Matt to get in the chair to save time. After it was all done and dusted, Matt stepped down and proudly stated, "Well I have now equalled in a couple of days what I had caught before we set off."

His three marlin had become six.

Well I'll be blowed, it was all happening on this trip.

With Matt, the man in charge of the lures, seemingly on cloud nine, I saw my opportunity.

The short corner had been quiet for a day or so, so I asked Mike to show me all his Wurzels. Some of the marlin we had caught had spewed arrow squid during the fight and nearly all of our bites had been on squid patterns, two in particular. Most of Mike's Wurzels were Kona-headed, high actioned, blue marlin specials but two caught my eye.

"I'll ask Matt to rig this one up and we'll replace the Rat," I said, but Mike didn't seem hopeful.

"Let's give the Rat a rest Matt, it seems better later on anyway, and run

"A 'plastic bag', the fishy type. Our fourth shortbilled spearfish of the season."

this for a bit."

"It hasn't got any orange in it," protested Matt.

"Neither has the Rat," I was ready for that one.

"OK, I'll rig it up."

"Need any help?"

"No. No, I'll do it right now."

Blimey that was easier than I expected.

The Wurzel was rigged and the Rat was recovered to await the evening bite when its darker colours seemed to be more effective.

At one thirty a marlin appeared behind the long corner, whacked it out, dropped back, came back into the spread, whacked the Wurzel on the short corner and was gone.

Ten minutes later, maybe the same fish came up again on the long corner, came in and hovered under the Wurzel before turning and eating the long rigger, this time to its cost and a fish of 110 kilos, number twenty for me was duly tagged.

Five minutes after its release another fish appeared behind the Wurzel, it messed around for ages and was gone.

Matt smiled and sharpened the hook on the Rat.

It remained quiet for nearly an hour.

The captain leaned over from his pulpit. "How many livebaits have we got?"

"Why we're doing fine with the lures?"

"I've told them we've caught a few on livebaits, we've got company on the way."

I checked.

The crays had seen to most of them. We had five semi-comatose koheru and a bunch of small street-wise Whangaroa Harbour jacks, ready for anything.

At three fifteen two barely swimming baits were lowered over the side and encouraged to move away from the boat. One was eaten immediately by a small mako. As the other was being retrieved a marlin cruised up and pinched the bait from the hook. As I dealt to the mako another bait was quickly lip-hooked and lowered over, only for it to be pinched again.

We tagged my mako quickly and got another, properly rigged bait out. Before the last livebait could be rigged and sent to its doom, a monster mako charged in and ate the one in the water.

The competition had turned up in time to see the first one tagged and the sight of the second, cartwheeling with gay abandon across their bow, was enough to send them away again.

"Yeah all sharks, can't shake them off, following us around. You should have stayed where you were," advised the skipper earnestly.

"Yeah, OK John, good luck, eh? See you later."

This mako had definitely been there before. For the first time I had one go down and dog unmercifully. I went to sunset, stood up and "sat" on the fish.

"Come on John, get it over with, it's nearly bite time," urged the captain, impatiently.

"What's up with him?"

"Well it's nearly four o'clock."

"Oh, crikey! I can't miss ten past!"

Shit or bust and it was bust, the shark bit through the line.

Any other time and I would have loved to complete the job, it was a real big one but there was no way it could ever have compensated for what came next and something I might have missed if I had delayed any longer.

The lures were out and it was ten past four, on the bloody dot and we were on a double!

It might briefly have been a treble but when I got down to business Mike looked across at me, an ambivalent look in his eye and said.

"I hope you picked the right one."

"Eh, what do you mean?"

"Look."

I looked. I was on the short corner. It was the Wurzel!

Oh man! The Wurzel.

It had raised fish non-stop, in the spot that had been quiet for a while and I was hooked-up to a big fish that I dare not lose.

Please God, I can't lose this one, this one is important, more than You could ever know. Well I suppose You do know, being omniscient and all that. Anyway let's get this one, eh?

Of course it was Matt on the other one and he soon disappeared around the boat, heading for the bow as I struggled to get some sort of control over mine. I can't remember if it jumped at any time, if it did I didn't see it. After its first tremendous rush it just dogged down and would not cooperate at all.

Grey would have referred to it as "a contrary fellow", Hemingway "a real S.O.B."

I had to agree with Hemingway.

We had to fish from a dead boat as I had loads of line out and Matt was apparently nearly spooled.

It was time to be patient.

"What the bloody hell is happening?" I implored of Mike.

"Just settle down, just make line when you can, I'll go and see how Matt is getting on."

Five minutes later they both reappeared and Matt completed his first circuit of the boat, we exchanged grimaces and he was off again on his next circumnavigation.

The time passed, my fish was down deep, a long way off and feeling heavy. It was like my worst broadbill moments, I felt powerless.

Matt came around again looking sunburned, hot and wobbly.

"How are you getting on Matt?"

"This fish is amazing, it jumps its arse off, takes a rest and goes at it again. It's jumped clean round the boat twice and I must have 800 yards of line out!"

"That's encouraging then, I'm not making much progress either."

"See you later." Matt was off again.

"Hey John is that Matt's fish jumping out there to our starboard? Over by that current line," I was looking at a commotion in the water.

The skipper took a look.

"No. Bloody hell! No, it's a pack of marlin, feeding right by the boat."

I couldn't believe it. What a place this is!

After half an hour I still hadn't found any patience and decided to make my dash for the line. I went into one-to-one on the reel and began pulling a dead weight inch-by-inch, gradually building up the spool.

"This fish is dead," I wailed.

"No it isn't, keep going," ordered the captain.

"Can you help me out?"

"No Matt hasn't got enough line to play with, you have to get yours first."

So I kept going. It was painful. For twenty minutes or so it was murder. I leaned into the weight of the fish and continued to slowly draw it towards me.

"It's got to be dead."

"No it isn't, we're still going ahead at nearly one and a half knots. This fish is still trucking!"

I couldn't believe that either.

The Dacron loop came onto the reel, it was the short so there wasn't much more to go.

"I can see it," cried the captain, "it's lit up and trucking."

I continued to quietly draw it in and I could see a big shape, pectorals flared and glowing. The skipper flew down the stairs to help Mike out. I drew the leader into Mike's hands and the big man had the bill in his vice.

"Come and see this John," said the skipper, "It's a bloody blue. It's a blue!"

I jumped out of the chair, legs like jelly and took a look.

It was lying by the boat. It was magnificent. Everything about it was perfect. It had more life glowing in it than I had. The hook was precariously caught in the top of its dorsal fin and a large hole had been worn out. The hook fell out as the line went slack.

It was truly magnificent. It was lit up and unbelievably unfazed by its hour-long cruise. Before I could go and get my camera, it made off, powering away and slipping down, whence it came.

I looked up in a daze to see Matt making his way back into the cockpit, looking very much worse for wear, sunburned and parched.

"I saw it, 200–220?" asked Matt.

"Yup," said the skipper, "all of 220 kilos. Let's go get yours."

"Thanks," was all Matt could muster.

Ten minutes later, his striped marlin of 120 kilos all but forgotten in my excitement and still putting up a fight was tagged, most perfectly again, by yours truly.

Well I'd done it, I'd caught another New Zealand blue marlin and amazingly exactly one year after I'd caught the last one, almost to the minute. It wasn't a giant, probably close to 500 pounds and certainly not the biggest I had encountered but nevertheless I danced a jig on the deck and all the aches and pains disappeared momentarily as I bathed in my own smug self-satisfaction.

"The Wurzel did it Mike! It's on the first team rota now buddy!"

"Maybe."

There's no pleasing some people.

He was putting the lures back out. It was five thirty.

At five forty five a fish took a shot at the short corner and went away. It came back, grabbed the Wurzel and pulled it out a few metres before shooting over and eating the long rigger. It jumped like a lunatic only for me to pull the hook out as I drew the leader to the boat. I wasn't unhappy. It could so easily have happened to the blue only half an hour earlier.

Nothing could upset me now. I was in Heaven.

At six fifteen a marlin appeared behind the long corner before weaving over and hitting the Wurzel on the short. This lure was hot!

The fish tore off, made one jump and was gone.

At seven o'clock, with all eyes on the short corner a good mako piled on the long corner and I put it to the sword in short order and another mako of 150 kilos was added to the tally.

This continuing frenzied effort however, had taken its toll, we had not had time to eat and I was feeling weak, seeing stars and there was a disturbing metallic taste in my mouth and it wasn't the Steinlager.

"Mike, I've had enough, I can't play any more today. I want you to play the next one from the chair."

"No, I won't do it."

"Yes you will. I'll tell the others I'm done for."

At a quarter to eight there was a massive crash on the short corner and the line raced away as the reel screeched like never before.

"Go on Mike, it's yours, it's eaten your Wurzel."

Reluctantly pushing up the drag Mike got in the chair and got to work.

There was an explosion out behind the boat and I heard the captain mutter something I couldn't quite catch. Within a few minutes what he'd said was revealed to all when the biggest mako you ever saw did a double somersault before crashing back and leaving a hole the boat could fall into.

Mike, for once enjoying the comfort of the chair, was working hard and making great strides.

"Push the drag up," urged the captain, "let's get back to the marlin fishing."

Poor Mike, he wasn't allowed his fun. Drag duly pushed up he bullied the shark to the boat. Matt was ready to take the leader and I was sort of ready with the tag pole.

"Really punch it home John and then run away quick." advised the skipper, barely disguising a scornful chortle.

"I'll be OK," I said bravely, looking at the short stout shark tag pole and wishing it was ten feet longer.

Matt heaved on the leader and the shark came up.

"It's hooked on the outside of its face," cried Matt as the shark shot round the back of the boat dragging Matt with it.

"It's gonna pull any second."

And it did.

Mike didn't take it very well. He remained on thirteen marlin and the Wurzel had taken a battering and needed some attention. The Rat got to go back out again and Matt unrigged the Wurzel and threw it on the bench with an air of finality.

At eight twenty five, we got a double on the long corner and the long rigger. I made Mike take the long rigger; the drop-back would give him a better chance of a hook-up. I got mine of 130 kilos in four minutes. Mike's jumped off.

Oh, dear.

At eight forty the lures were back out and it was nearly dark.

At nine o'clock a big blue marlin monstered the lumo on the long rigger and disappeared into the night.

I got in the chair. I couldn't see a thing; thank goodness it was only a single.

As the lures were cleared and the boat stopped before backing up after the marlin, loud splashes could be heard in the blackness. The rod unloaded and the fish was gone.

We'd been on the go for fourteen hours, we hadn't gone a single hour without playing a fish, we'd had twenty-five bites and caught five striped marlin, one blue marlin and five mako sharks. We'd played seven more, three of which were lost at the boat, nothing was less than 100 kilos and the boat was on twenty-seven marlin for the trip. By any standards it was amazing fishing and tomorrow we got the chance to do it all again.

We drifted five miles overnight so it took a while to get back to our hot spot; even so the lures were in the water at six forty-five.

At eight thirty I caught a small yellowfin tuna that Mike wanted for the galley but I insisted it was tagged much to the bemusement of the rest of the happy band of warriors.

"I'm not killing the first fish of the day, it's bad luck and not good form," was all I had to say on the matter.

Fifteen minutes later, as if to prove my point, we were pack attacked and three striped marlin were firmly hooked-up. Mike's was a really big fish that jumped clear out and put the other two to shame.

Mine was the smallest at 90 kilos and as we were getting better at this now, I got it quickly and Matt's was soon to follow even though he had done his usual trip round the boat before I got the tag in it.

We'd done it; number twenty-nine was in the bag!

All eyes were now on Mike who was going well and the fish was coming nicely, there was no rush. The skipper could see the fish from his elevated position and the wind on was out of the water. Matt leaned forward to collect it.

Then the hook pulled out.

The fish was just there, it was free to go but it lingered tantalisingly out of reach before gliding gently away.

There was no point in trying to console Mike, he was way past that point and I offered him the tag pole and suggested he do the decent thing. Hara Kiri, that was all that was left for the poor bugger.

The lures were out again at nine thirty-five, at nine-forty a big stripey of at least 130 kilos smashed the lure and careered around, jumping like crazy. It was less than fifty metres away and in its frantic struggle had become totally wrapped up in the leader. This was going to be a very easy one, the simplest catch imaginable. The other lures were in and we had just begun to go and get it when the marlin reared up out of the water. I could see its head and shoulders pointing towards the Heavens and a great grey shape appeared beneath it. The rod bucked in my hands, the marlin shuddered and a great pool of blood spread out all around it. The line went slack. It was bitten through like the wrapped up marlin, its colour immediately extinguished and the whitening fish slowly subsided beneath the surface.

The marlin had been eaten by a great white shark.

From his elevated position above me the captain had witnessed the incredible incident in its entirety and was visibly shocked by what he had seen, as indeed were we all, and I don't think it was because he'd lost over two hundred dollars of lure and rigging.

The whole thing had only taken 3–4 minutes, the marlin seemingly devoured in two monstrous bites.

We later guessed that the shark had been on the fish from the outset and was why the big stripey had behaved so oddly. I could only imagine what might have occurred if the marlin had not been wrapped in the line, the shark had not bitten through the leader and I had attempted to wind in only the head and shoulders after the shark's first attack.

In all respects we were quiet for a couple of hours as the sad episode sank in.

At midday, I got the next bite.

I left the drag really light as the fish jumped around, it stayed on the surface after settling down and we crept over as I wound and wound and it was collected, tagged – maybe 90 kilos and sent on its way.

As though the Bank and the fish knew that this was our last day the action slowed to a more reasonable pace so we could come down slowly from the highs we had enjoyed.

It wasn't until nearly three in the afternoon that the next marlin appeared. I used the light drag approach again, which was perfect until Mike grabbed the leader and the fish went berserk. The gel coat took a battering and the skipper tore down in a bit of a paddy and lifted a seriously surprised 120 kilo marlin almost above his head, the necessary formalities were completed and the grateful fish was "turned loose" a bit further from the hull than usual.

The afternoon wore on and I spotted the Wurzel, unrigged and looking forlorn on the bench.

"Come on Matt, let's cheer up poor old Mike."

"Yeah, why not."

The Rat came in at six thirty having completed its shift and the Wurzel looking very smart was back in its rightful place on the short corner where it ducked and dived and smoked and looked happy.

Well it cheered me up anyway.

At a quarter to eight a small striped marlin came up behind it.

The dorsal went up and down and quivered.

"What are you waiting for? Eat the bloody thing."

The fish dropped back slightly then charged forward, wagging its bill frantically and whacking the lure.

I was right there, a few metres away, watching it all.

The fish turned and the line whizzed out. I knew that it hadn't eaten the lure; I guessed it was bill-wrapped but I kept it to myself.

"Push the drag up! Push the drag up!" Matt was beside himself.

"It's OK. I know what I'm doing."

I let the fish turn away until it was running directly away from the boat and I very gently began collecting the line as the captain eased the boat after the fish. I was sure he knew what I knew. The fish stayed on the surface and hounded away as we slalomed around to keep behind it. I was getting line all the time and we were getting closer and closer.

"You need to get the drag up, don't get a slack line."

"OK," I said, ignoring him and continuing as before.

I could see the wind on coming and the un-panicked fish was swimming away nicely.

"Just pinch the leader Mike, wait until Matt's got the tag in."

"You sure?"

The fish came up and its back was out of the water as I collected more line and the boat bore down on it. Matt plunged forward and stuck the tag right on the spot.

Mike eased the fish around to the portside.

"It's bill-wrapped," shouted Mike, "It's barely locked on, look at that!"

He lifted the leader, the fish had slipped out of the loop and was gliding away, free and unharmed.

The capture of this particular fish, in such circumstances, was a great

"We had tagged thirty-two marlin including twenty-six for me, all in a week."

personal achievement for me and was a most satisfying moment.

We had tagged thirty-two marlin including twenty-six for me, all in a week.

I raised the lure.

"Look at that Matt, Mike's Wurzel did it again!"

"Yeah, but it still hasn't hooked anything in the gob."

Eldorado Revisited

When the incomparable Zane Grey was invited to New Zealand by its Government in 1926, he could not have imagined that his fishing would be so successful.

His reputation battered in the USA after being forced to resign from the Avalon Tuna Club in 1921 for disparaging a fellow lady member's capture of a 426lb broadbill swordfish, which happened to be 8lb bigger than his own of the previous season, he had become somewhat embittered and was no doubt glad to get away from the jealous and poisonous recriminations in which he had become embroiled back in California.

He was, by 1926, the world's foremost heavy tackle fisherman and the adventurer and his party arrived after recent successful trips to Nova Scotia (1924), and Cocos Island, the Galapagos, and the Mexican west coast (1925). He came as the holder of the world record for bluefin tuna 758lb, Pacific sailfish 135lb and yellowfin tuna 315lb. He had also helped his brother Romer ("R.C.") to the record striped marlin 354lb. "R.C." was the only man to have caught more than one striped marlin over 300lb and by 1924 had caught five.

In his 1926 catch of 42 marlin in the Bay of Islands, New Zealand, Zane Grey caught seven over 300lb and a "black" (so named by Grey) marlin of 704lb. His fishing companion, Captain Laurie Mitchell who had never previously caught a marlin before but had once held the bluefin tuna record of 710lb, caught four over 300lb plus two black marlin of 685lb and the record 976lb. In Grey's employ, Mitchell fished with him through to the early 1930s when after a serious dispute in Tahiti, Grey fired him and they never fished together again.

1926 was a monumental year for Zane Grey, as immediately after *"around 110 kilos, it was the magnificent 42 and a fantastic way to catch it."*

returning to Avalon and Catalina Island from his expedition to New Zealand, he confounded his critics by capturing a new record broadbill swordfish at 582lb after a five and half hour battle. He and "R.C." caught ten broadbill on returning to California that year, five each, including a 515 pounder.

Grey had been so impressed by the fishing in New Zealand he returned privately the following year with his 190 foot, three-masted schooner, *The Fisherman* and a full complement of equipment and guests. However, maybe because of poor weather and rough seas, he was unable to reproduce a similar result and his angler return of 42 marlin in 1926 appears to have remained a record for a season in New Zealand.

In 2003, after tagging and releasing 26 marlin in one week in February on New Zealand's famed King Bank, I reckoned that emulating Grey, whose exploits I had admired for so long, would be something worth trying for.

By the time I had returned from a two-week trip in March I had lifted my season's total to 39, all on lures and each one tagged and released, so it was with great excitement that in April I took off again in search of the three marlin to equal Zane Grey's wonderful effort of all those years ago.

This seven-day trip was going to be my last of the season and on the 19th of April I was again on board *Primetime* with skipper John Gregory with a few extra beers in case I had cause to celebrate. I had kept quiet about my hopes for the trip, for fear of ridicule but when I learned that we were going to use a "tease and switch" method and remove the hooks from the big short lures I began to get anxious.

The marlin had been finicky of late and seemingly reluctant to eat lures readily, so the captain's plan was to tease the fish in close, get it over-excited and then pitch it a dead-bait. Now, any marlin, no matter how caught, would be great but I was hoping to go through the season with all marlin caught on lures, Grey's were all on baits and were all strung up, mine were all going to be tagged and released regardless of any circumstance barring dead-on-arrival. With two hook-less lures in the water my chances were halved and restricted to the smaller lures run off the riggers.

We left Whangaroa in fair weather and other than the sight of a couple of tailing marlin we remained undisturbed and went into North Cape for the night. The reports from The Three Kings were not good, the water was green and cold according to the boats on the King Bank and the

Middlesex Bank and nothing had been caught up there for days. We had had some good sport fishing the Hook and the Fingers north of North Cape and even at the Compass Rose on the way to the King Bank on my previous trip in March but again the area had gone quiet after some rough weather and the guess was that the bait schools had been broken up and the marlin were scattered or had gone down and were feeding below the thermocline.

So on the second day we headed out to the Garden Patch instead and first thing, before we had gone too far I was lucky to hook into a good fish as we crossed the Parengarenga Canyons. By keeping the drag light the fish stayed on top after it's initial thrash around and jumping about and we crept over and collected it in our inimitable way and the tag was pushed into a nice fish of around 125 kilos after a controlled 15 minute contest.

As is often the case with an early fish, it was barely 8am, we saw nothing for the rest of the day barring a bunch of aggressive orcas and we worked back to North Cape and our anchorage.

Undecided about our next move we fished above North Cape the next day and worked the Hook and the Fingers with one eye on the Three Kings to the west of us. I dropped a striped marlin after a half-hearted bite and the pressure to tease and switch became even stronger. Suddenly, in the middle of the afternoon with everything quiet, the skipper gave the order to pull the gear and we were soon steaming towards the King Bank.

A boat fishing there had reported an improvement in the water colour and that was all he needed to hear.

When we arrived the water was green and over a degree colder than that we had left.

"If this is bluer water, I can't imagine what it was like before!" The skipper was not impressed.

However, within minutes we had a fish up but no strike, just a looker and it disappeared as quickly as it had arrived. It was enough though for us to stay on the Bank until nearly dark before we ran up to the broadbill grounds and began towing a skirted squid.

Not long after dinner we got bit and I settled into the chair and felt the immense weight of an unseen fish that did not know it was hooked. It stayed with the boat and I was collecting line quite easily until the fish suddenly woke up. The fish leaned heavily against me and I could do nothing more but hold on as it powered away. With the drag well over the button the fish was still taking line easily and unstoppably. I grasped the base of the fighting chair with one hand and standing up on the footrest, I leaned back and let the fish do the work.

But the hook pulled out.

As I got out of the chair after my five minutes of heroics, the skipper said that the boat next to us had hooked-up at the same time and they were still on their fish.

"Oh well, good luck to them." I wasn't sure if I really meant it, but still.

When we pulled the gear at dawn to return to marlin fishing, they were still on their fish.

Later, after ten hours they got the broadbill to the boat and the hook pulled out.

I reckon I got the better deal.

So, day four, on the King Bank, hooks removed from the shorts and the pitch-bait ready to pitch.

It was dead.

We saw nothing until at five o'clock, out of nowhere, it had not even shown on the sounder, a meatball popped up thirty metres behind the boat, right in the middle of our spread and as we all watched disbelievingly, a big striped marlin leaped straight out of the centre of the meatball, completely clear of the surface like a missile and gave us a two-fingered salute. It hung high in the air, lit-up, stripes blazing and shining in the westering sun and crashed back into the bait and it all disappeared like magic.

We turned back to find nothing on the sounder, not a scratch; if we hadn't all seen it I'd have said it was a mirage.

We sword-fished until three in the morning and then steamed back towards North Cape and the Fingers to see if there would be an early marlin bite back in the better water.

When the sun came up we knew the skipper had made the right call yet again. The colour was good and it was warmer.

We worked back to the Hook outside on the 200 metre line.

We were in the area where a number of blue marlin had been reported in previous weeks. I just prayed that a big blue, something I had been longing for, didn't pile on to our hook-less "Smokin' Joe".

As I was thinking this both riggers popped and the reels began singing.

I could tell almost immediately that I wasn't into a marlin and I looked anxiously across to the deckhand who was playing the other one. I needn't have worried as we both brought in identical 15 kilo yellowtail kingfish that scrapped as best they could on the 37 kilo outfits before being tagged and unhooked.

The day wore on.

Other boats came and went, everyone searching and hoping but not finding the fish. We had been at sea for nearly five days and had only tagged one marlin; I felt we were running out of time.

Prior to the rough weather, which preceded this trip, there had been big schools of mackerel in the same area and the Hawaiian "Evil" lure had been a killer for us, getting seven out of eight marlin in three days. It was out now on the short rigger behind it's big brother the "Smokin'

"the Hawaiian "Evil" lure had been a killer for us, getting seven out of eight marlin in three days."

Joe" which was running as a teaser. On the long side was a yellowish jack mackerel imitator as a teaser with another handcrafted blue mackerel lure on the long rigger. Also waiting on the long side, and probably the wrong side, was the soft and ageing mackerel pitch bait, rigged on a 24 kilo outfit.

Late in the afternoon, nearing five o'clock a marlin appeared from nowhere and launched itself at the short rigger. I was looking at the "Evil" when it happened, the take was instantaneous and the line poured off the reel in a satisfactory manner. Luckily, like our first and only other marlin of the trip, the fish didn't panic, didn't sound and was obviously not feeling the hook. I eased the line back onto the reel as we quietly got closer and with the fish idling away on the surface it was leadered gently and tagged with the minimum of fuss and maximum efficiency. As more weight was applied to turn the fish for unhooking, it rolled around and the hook, which was looped over the bill, slipped off and the marlin swam away unconcerned.

Number 41 and a good job by all involved, ensured we were lucky in getting the bill-wrapped fish to the boat successfully.

Things were looking up; maybe it was going to happen after all.

With the gear back in the water we turned back to where we had hooked-up.

A marlin cruised in and whacked the jack mackerel lure on the long corner and then swayed across to the "Smokin' Joe" and tried to eat it as the mate pulled it away. The fish then dropped back and had a crack at the "Evil". All the time I was trying to get it interested in the rotten mackerel that was skipping at lure speed in the white prop wash. The bait dropped back towards the "Evil" and the fish grabbed the bait but dropped it again quickly as the mate pulled the lure away and the fish, much more interested in the lure, tried to eat it. My bait was mangled but as I let it fall back, past the marlin's eye, the fish turned, grabbed it and took off. After it had run about 100 metres I eased up the drag and pulled the bait out of its jaws. I cranked the reel bringing the remains of the bait back to the surface and the marlin came back again, took one look at the smashed bait hanging off the hook and disappeared.

Not an impressive start with the pitch bait, number 42 was going to be a problem.

With everything reset, only this time with the pitch bait on the short side so it could be run back on the hot side of the boat without the chair and the prop wash getting in the way, my eyes were firmly fixed again on the magic lure on the short rigger and I prayed again that the next fish, if there was to be one, would just tear in and eat it.

At six o'clock another striped marlin surfaced and it was all over the place attacking everything in the spread and the deck was alive with bodies, teasing and cranking and shouting and cursing. I made straight for the "Evil" and popped the rigger and wound the lure back towards the boat. The fish was frantic, careering around trying to eat the lot and as the mate pitched the bait and before the marlin could find it, I fed it the "Evil" and it hoovered it in just perfectly.

We had a fast and furious scrap but with the marlin securely hooked right through its bottom jaw there could only be one outcome and after some spectacular surface action, this fish was definitely feeling the hook, it was mine. Similar size to the previous one, around 110 kilos, it was the magnificent 42 and a fantastic way to catch it.

Feeling very proud of myself and glowing inside, I grabbed a beer and saluted the sky.

"See you up there some day! I'll tell you what you could have done with hooks in your teasers, or even outriggers! You would have loved tag and release!"

I turned round to be greeted by some quizzical looks of astonishment.

I couldn't have given a hoot; I was in another place and danced a little jig on the deck.

I hadn't really considered exceeding the magic 42, I was extremely happy to have matched it and could have quite joyfully gone home at that moment, but we weren't done yet.

Just before dark the "Evil" got bit again. The fish took some line and the reel began the ominous "zip", "zip", "zip" as the marlin sat there shaking its head from side to side trying to get rid of the hook. I got the drag up quickly to try and set the hook and pinned it right through the bill. Suddenly aware that the game was up, the fish took off in total panic and dragged us into the moonlight before a really stubborn 120 kilo striped marlin became number 43.

Nearly five days for one and then three in less than two hours, just by being in the right place at the right time.

What a captain!

The other boats had come and gone but he'd stuck it out, knowing that the fish were there and just waiting for bite time.

We ran back to Tom Bowling Bay for the night but were away again before daylight to get back to the hot spot to see if there would be an early bite as well as the late one we had been lucky enough to experience.

It was barely light at 7am and we had a double on.

I had seen a dorsal pop up behind the long rigger but a couple of minutes had passed with no strike. I was about to stand down and then it hit the fan.

At least three fish were in the spread and it was pandemonium.

I had to make a fast choice, bait or lure? What should I do?

The mate fed the pitch-bait and it was eaten immediately.

He handed me the rod but I didn't really want to take it, the fish was on, would I have to disqualify it?

The decision was made for me when another marlin took off with the long rigger and the mate struck the fish.

So here we were, I was into a fish that had eaten a bait.

Blast!

I knew I had chosen wrongly and to confirm my fear, the fish threw the hook and I let the mate climb into the chair.

These guys are often full of it when the angler is hooked-up, screaming advice or complaining about inadequacies in technique or style, but it is amazing how the confidence can drain away when it's down to them.

Time dragged on as he nervously played the fish, not daring to apply too much pressure for fear of losing it but eating up valuable bite-time as we moved further away from the hot spot.

I can't say I was happy but hey-ho, "I'll get over it" and sure enough an hour or so later, after I had tagged the marlin for him, I got another chance.

I didn't screw around with the pitch-bait this time.

After the fish was teased to distraction I fed it the lure again and Bingo! Number 44 was chalked up before we had to begin to work our way around North Cape and home, back to Whangaroa, "where sweet content her harbour holds".

In 1926 Zane Grey had caught 41 striped marlin and a black marlin as well as a broadbill swordfish and a number of smallish mako sharks.

I actually ended up with 44 striped marlin and a blue marlin as well as a broadbill swordfish and some big makos. I had also tagged some short-billed spearfish; a beautiful-looking fish Grey would not have known existed.

Interestingly the average size of our striped marlin was very similar, just above 115 kilos (250lb), as also was the amount of 300lb plus fish.

So maybe not much has really changed in over 75 years of big game fishing these New Zealand shores.

I'm sure Zane Grey would love to come back for a visit, I shall tell him all about it when I see him.

The Nationals

Fishing! Some things change, some never change. The things we would prefer didn't, usually do and mainly as a result of our own actions and the things that never change are out of our control anyway and no matter what we do they will persist. Fishing is an ageless pastime but big game fishing is a relatively young sport of barely a hundred years and gamefishing the Oceans is even more recent but in those intervening years how we have changed things.

From the pioneering days of the early 1900s when the seas were teeming and seemingly inexhaustible, to what we have today when early each season the questions are asked, "Will they come?"

"Will the yellowfin tuna turn up, will the blue marlin return with them?" "Will the skipjack arrive?" "When will the striped marlin get here…?"

Well, I confess, I sometimes despair of the marlin fishing in New Zealand; I just can't work it out. In December 2002 and January 2003 the marlin just didn't appear and after making such elaborate plans, I had scoured the ocean in vain. Days and days and thousands of nautical miles for naught. In January 2004 when I had scaled down my fishing effort, remembering the pitiful return of twelve months previous, the striped marlin were everywhere and in great numbers. The weather remained settled and those that ventured out, myself included, couldn't fail to catch a load of fish.

I hadn't been alone in scaling down my early fishing effort and most of the charter boats had very few bookings; *Primetime* had none in December and other than me, none in January. The private recreational boats had a ball and it was interesting to see the host of small runabouts zigzagging all over the place with guys hanging out the sides searching the calm surface for feeding, free-jumping or tailing marlin. I only got out for seven days but tagged thirteen off Whangaroa and the Cavallis where we were sometimes getting ten to twelve shots and we had some great, almost unheard of for the east coast, three and four fish days.

Unlike other years at this time, the fish were mainly in good condition and those that were, were fat and feisty and fought well and longer than any others I could recall. We only collected a few "industry standard" fish in ten to fifteen minutes and most took half an hour or more on 37 kilo outfits and still had plenty left when giving us a good show at the boat. To the captain's disdain the gel coat picked up some "bill rash" and the odd "signature" but as the tally mounted his humour returned and we enjoyed a happy ship and for the most part were too busy to remain affected by the odd mishap.

As January expired my thoughts turned to my next planned trip — the New Zealand Nationals.

Now I am not a great fan of tournament fishing, especially if it is geared to seeing the fish hanging at the weigh-station. Additionally, "One Base" tournaments where you have to return to the gamefish club each night to keep the bar takings up and unless you have the boat and the money to do a lot of high speed running before fishing starts in the morning and again at the end of the day in order to get back by the allotted time, the accessible fishing area can be very limited.

The eight day, twenty-four hour, New Zealand National Tournament, taking place during the last week of February is a different kettle of fish and as long as you remain within the 200 mile EEZ and are surveyed to go there, you can fish where you want. With 160 sections to compete for and up to 1000 contestants, it is the New Zealand season's premier event.

I had not entered before but taking part and hopefully winning the tagged marlin and billfish sections was one of my targets for the 2004 season. I also hoped that my thirteen-year-old son James would have a good chance of taking the respective Junior titles.

The conditions of the event pointed to using lighter tackle than I had become used to and if I was to gain maximum points from my marlin captures I would have to scale down from 37 kilo (80 pounds) to 15 kilo (30 pounds), a challenge in itself. Also there was a strong likelihood of "stand-up" fishing, yet another challenge, at least for the damaged knees and back.

As in previous years it was expected that the battle for major honours would be fought out on the banks near the Three Kings Islands north of Cape Reinga; either the King Bank as in the previous year, or the Middlesex Bank like the one before that; notwithstanding the fact that the marlin had already showed up in numbers all around the north of the North Island.

Incredibly on a short exploratory trip to the King Bank during the second week of February, John Gregory had taken *Primetime* with its disbelieving charter and tagged an amazing forty striped marlin in only four days including thirteen on the last day and some of them appeared to be close to the magical 200 kilo mark. (Only a handful have ever been recorded above this weight).

"I hope those big buggers have moved on by the Nationals," said the skipper to me on his return, "with multi-strikes of doubles and trebles they killed us on 37 kilo, we'd not have a hope on 15! Still, there were reports of tons of smaller fish on the Middlesex, maybe that's where we'll end up."

I didn't care where we went, I just wanted to get there and get stuck in.

The week before the Nationals was the Whangaroa "One Base" and as usual it was greeted by a severe deterioration in the weather. Twenty five to thirty five knots of mostly northerly winds, thunderstorms and heavy rain kept a lot of anglers in the harbour, or in the bar and I was glad that I had decided to sit this one out; all thoughts of forays to North Cape and beyond definitely on the back burner and I sat at home trying not to stew about it all and to get focussed on the task to come.

At least the week's fishing I had had in the middle of January meant that I wouldn't be going into the Nationals looking for my first fish, I already had thirteen marlin on my tally.

Thirteen.

Bloody thirteen.

At least I wouldn't be trying to catch number thirteen but like whistling Jonah's banana I would rather not be sailing with it, especially not on a Friday.

And then there was the weather.

Still, why should I worry? I was yet again on the "Hot Boat", but John Gregory had only added one more fish during the five-day "One Base" to *Primetime*'s impressive return, making 59 for a season that was merely six weeks old. He had, up until then, only fished 13 days for 58 fish and we are not talking 30 pound sailfish or 45 pound white marlin but striped marlin averaging 300 pounds.

But then there was the weather. As I said some things you can't change.

The fish might have been in abundance before, but the curse of the "One Base" had struck. Calm seas had given way to three metre swells and 35 knots of northeast winds switched back and forth with 35 knots of southwest as the fronts roared in on an endless conveyor belt, day after day with no end in sight and I sank into a miserable pit of despair.

A whole year in the planning and the New Zealand weather had reared up like it does and dumped me on my backside.

It was cold, wet, and windy. It was like winter. It was horrible.

There were two days to go before the off.

And it got worse.

The fishery had shut down, no marlin had been seen for five days, water that was once blue and 21°C was now green and as low as 16°C. The seas were whipped into a maelstrom of foaming spray pouring off the tops of huge grey swells.

We watched and watched the forecasts hoping that the high off Australia would build, instead it got squeezed up from the south and the wind blew and blew. It howled and the southern part of the North Island got hammered. Floods, storms; it was the worst for thirty years and the country was gripped by the shocking news images of landslips and houses and livestock being swept away by raging torrents of immense rivers of mud and debris.

There was no respite and none on the horizon.

What to do?

There was only one thing for it.

We went fishing.

If anyone said we were crazy I shouldn't complain.

What would be the point?

We had to play with the cards we were dealt but with no aces or faces in the pack, seven high was looking grim.

I had never left Whangaroa feeling less confident.

The cold and damp had got into my knees and I'd left my brave face tucked up in bed at home with the missus.

"We must be mad, going out in this shite!" Even Captain John, not

The Nationals | 153

"At this stage James had released six marlin, five on 15 kilo and had accrued 3400 points."

known to be the least faint-hearted, added to the air of futility.

"At least the sun's shining!" Perhaps I'd brought the brave face after all.

We crept out of the harbour after filling up on jack and slimy mackerel, turned left and felt our way up the coast, edging out to 120 metres and putting out the lures.

Doubtless Bay was a washing machine and Great Exhibition Bay was worse.

By the time we got to North Cape around four pm the water temperature had dropped to 15°C.

"OK. Pull the gear, we're out of here!"

We ran along the top of New Zealand to Cape Reinga, hugging the coast line and falling into a few holes on the way; holes that jarred the spine when the boat fell off the top of backless swells. At Cape Reinga, we held our breath, made the jump and headed out to the Johnson Trough and the Three Kings Islands beyond. Hopefully we'd be in North West Bay before eleven o'clock and get a good start in the morning. We were a day ahead of the rest of the fleet, lets hope we could take advantage of our brave move.

"Get everything tied down, the first couple of hours will be the worst after that it will only be bad. If the Trough is dogshit we'll turn back and try again in the morning."

The Johnson Trough can be a real pig at the best of times, even with little wind you can be climbing walls created by the strong tidal flows that pour round the top of New Zealand.

All the charts I'd looked at before leaving suggested that the further north we got the better it would be; with any luck we would be leaving the weather behind and the nasty lows being spawned in the Tasman would pester the South Island and leave us alone.

Let's face it, they deserve it.

I'd left the Three Kings with a forty knot forecast but never gone there with such a promise.

As it transpired the crossing was not too uncomfortable, we made good time and had the anchor down at nine thirty. The contents of the fuel bladder were pumped into the main fuel tanks and we were sitting at the Three Kings with full tanks, a clear deck and rising spirits.

Stage one was complete. Weather permitting our "Nationals" would begin in earnest at 8am.

That night, which turned out to be tedious and uncomfortable, the boat took up an attitude beam on to the swell and we rocked and rolled and slapped around and the crew took turns on anchor watch until it was with great relief that the motors were fired up just before six o'clock and we got under way.

Dawn broke with the sun, which stayed out all day and made the thirty knots and big swells more bearable.

We were alone on the King Bank.

Alone, other than the host of striped marlin that first put in an appearance at eight thirty, thirty minutes after the official start of the Tournament.

With the points for tagged marlin being 600 points on 15 kilo, 400 points on 24 kilo and 300 points on 37 kilo, we were running four lures, only one of which had a hook in it, the short rigger on a 24 kilo outfit, the rest were being run as teasers. The long rigger was run from the flybridge leaving the right side of the fighting chair free for the 15 kilo rigged pitch bait.

A strange set-up. How would we manage?

Not too good as it happened.

The first fish didn't get the idea of the "tease" and was not the least bit interested in the "switch" and after whacking the long corner five or six times, got bored and disappeared; closely followed by its buddy who whacked the long rigger a couple of times without knocking out of the rigger clip. The pitch bait in the meantime was not as much skipping or swimming as jumping and leaping about and was mainly airborne above the white prop wash.

It was a poor start and was repeated twice more with little success and increasing frustration until soon after lunch the fish got a bit more aggressive.

Another boat had turned up beside us and caught two marlin in quick succession.

The frustration grew but there was more to come.

Three times more we had doubles in the gear and trying to eat the teasers and the pitch bait was as pathetic as ever; the bait was too light and the sea too rough for it to be properly presented. We were missing our chances, if we didn't convert some of these opportunities soon, our one-day head start would be wasted.

I got to the chair twice before the fish escaped, James did once also with the same result before I finally hooked-up solid and bullied a small yellowfin to the tagpole.

A fish. I was grateful but it was the wrong sort.

Something had to be done.

At long last the pitch bait was scrapped, a hook was put in the lure on the long corner on a 15 kilo outfit and the pitch bait became a pitch lure instead, something that would swim and not leap about and the same pattern as the teaser on the short corner, the position where a lot of enquiries had been made.

It's a pity that nobody had seen fit to tell Sean.

Sean was the number two deckhand, an amiable sort, quite a character.

However, when the next fish swept in, shortly thereafter and nailed the now hooked long corner, Sean swept in and swept up the drag and drove the hook nicely into the marlin's jaw.

"Sorry mate, I thought it was a teaser."

Oh dear!

Now was the time to be philosophical, but why be philosophical when you can be bitter and twisted.

He got the fish.

I was glad he got the fish but then I'd have been glad if he'd lost it.

After a few more failed attempts I gave up and handed primary hooking duties to James and blow me down if the next fish didn't hook-up well and James steered his first marlin of the Nationals to the boat, doing well on the, easy to handle, 15 kilo set-up.

It was getting late in the day but there was still time for a few more halfhearted chances but with no joy.

Every dog has its day. Today I was not going to be the dog.

I was still stuck on thirteen but better must come? There was plenty of time and we had the ability to get a bunch of fish very quickly. My luck would improve; I just had to be patient. Relax, have a beer. Stay calm.

Bloody Sean! Rotten fish stealing smeg-head. "Sorry mate, thought it was a teaser."

Yeah, right.

Relax, plenty of time. I'll get my just desserts.

And I did, the next day.

By the next day the main fleet began to arrive in earnest and nearly all of them went to the Middlesex Bank and left us alone. We had stayed out and drifted that night, it was a bit lumpy but not as bad as the first night at anchor at the Three Kings and it paid off because by nine o'clock we had nailed three marlin from three bites, two to me on 24 kilo and one to James on 15 kilo. I even got another at eleven thirty, again on 24 kilo, bringing my points score to 1200 the same as James with his two fish on 15 kilo. With six fish we were now leading the field and just had to maintain consistency to stay in front.

Later in the day I tagged another yellowfin but then our chances dried up and we began to hear about the boats on the Middlesex running over a bunch of fish on the way back to the Islands. Doubles, trebles, everyone getting in on the action but with few fish getting to the boat successfully. Nevertheless we now had some real competition and if the fish were

"jumped high and thrashed its head, showing us all of its repertoire"

there for them in the numbers it appeared we would have to pull out all the stops to keep ahead.

We stayed out again that night and the sea had settled down a lot and for the first time we all got a fair night's sleep.

The lures were out at seven am and at seven thirty James got the first marlin of the day, again on 15 kilo before, for a while, it went quiet.

"Sorry mate."

Sean had been hovering in the background for the last day or so, head bowed and repeating "Sorry mate" everytime our eyes met. I wasn't letting him off the hook yet and just growled a bit and watched him wince.

The boats on the Middlesex had found the fish again in the same place as the night before and were filling their boots. One boat, *Independence*, actually ended the day with six, most of which were to a junior angler but we didn't know that until later in the evening when the roll call was made back to Far North Radio, who were listening in and reporting the catches back to our respective Gamefishing Clubs.

But we kept our tally ticking over, me with another small yellowfin and then James with yet another marlin on 15 kilo at lunchtime, one of a double that were both hooked well and after successfully releasing James' fish we went after mine, which gave us an exciting display near the boat. Three times it powered away and jumped high and thrashed its head, showing us all of its repertoire before digging in a bit and breaking the leader at the boat before we could get the tag in.

A big disappointment but also one of the hot lures had gone too but at last I finally managed to nail the bogey and got a marlin myself on 15 kilo in the middle of the afternoon and marvelled at how easy it was.

As the evening approached the fish were being called in to the roll call and it became apparent that we were not having it all our own way, we may have been ahead on numbers of fish but I had three of mine on 24 kilo. All the other boats were fishing 15 kilo exclusively and their points were mounting.

We needed more fish and soon we were on a double.

Both James and I stayed in the stand up harnesses as the marlin were close to the boat and really active. Twice we had to cross and duck around each other as our fish converged and jumped around; my fish actually jumped over the line of the lure still up in the long rigger before arcing back around to jump up the port side of the boat. With James leaning out of the starboard side the skipper spun the boat in order to get onto mine but it jumped and spat the hook with the double line nearly on the rod. We were that close.

After that James was able to get in the chair and soon brought his fish in to be tagged.

So at the end of the third day we had released ten marlin, five to James and four to me but James was way ahead on points so it seemed a good idea to promote him up the strike order, especially as the leading angler from the other boats was a junior too.

The other boat, *Independence*, that had caught six for the day, had decided to take a marlin back to weigh at Houhoura, it would take them a day to get there and back, if we could have another good day tomorrow, we could take advantage of their absence.

As it happened we got another chance right on dark at nine o'clock as we began to run back to the Islands for a change of venue in the morning.

We saw the marlin in the gloom come and monster the teaser on the short corner but then another fish grabbed the lure on the rigger on the same side and took off at great speed.

I went to the chair and fought the fish in the glare of the decklights.

We were all disappointed when the culprit, a mako of about 150 kilos appeared at the boat but also amazed that it was feeding with a stripey!

We crept into North West Bay and got the anchor down by eleven o'clock. It was pretty packed but the wind had dropped away and it had been misty all day with the fog coming and going in varying degrees of thickness. Fog that had caused for some interesting moments for all the boats fighting over the same patch of water on the south western edge of the Middlesex Bank and where the action had been for them for the last two days; particularly early and late in the day.

Well our plan was to get going early and if it was still foggy we would return to the King Bank, if not we would join the ranks and show them what we could do. It also made anyone think twice about venturing over to the King Bank, if it were so good why would we leave it? Why indeed?

Also we could always wander up to the top of the Middlesex Bank where nobody had spent any time yet, it might be a bit rough up there but if all went well we could get another four or five or even more if we got lucky.

We were up again before six am and slipped quietly away. The fog had gone, the wind had increased a bit but it was fine. There were still the big swells to contend with but it was fishable with ease.

We worked around the hot spot where they had been getting all their bites and before long the other boats began to join us. One boat got a fish but other than that it was quiet.

So we gradually worked our way up to the top of the Middlesex where the bait was piled high, the water was blue and the marlin came to play.

But that's all they did do, play.

It was tease and switch, but the fish were doing the teasing.

We must have seen a dozen or more fish but only got one bite, which didn't stick.

We were in the right place at the wrong time. It was going to go off but not today.

The fish were obviously fed up and full, not in the mood to eat plastic.

They certainly were back where we had started the day, the late bite had begun and one boat, *Striker*, and now our main rival had tagged six fish, we had caught none and were getting worried.

We began the run back but were pushing more than two knots of tide and were making slow headway, it would be all over before we got back. We had blown it and wasted a day. The mood in the camp was decidedly iffy.

Just as well that, as we came up to the Princes Island Group just a few miles from the anchorage, we got a bite right on sunset. I know because we were filming it sink into a flaming sea and disappear with a flash below the horizon when we got the Shimano wake up call.

I had told James that the next few fish were his and he duly did his duty and quickly brought the bemused marlin to the boat in the dark. Like makos at night this fish had no idea what was going on and was led like a puppy around the boat and tagged and released with the absolute minimum of fuss.

So a day that had promised much and delivered little had finally ended in smiles and the nervousness of a few minutes previous had blossomed into a renewed determination.

At this stage James had released six marlin, five on 15 kilo and had accrued 3400 points. I had released four for the meagre total of 1800 points. The expectation was that James was leading the field by maybe a fish or two and that team *Primetime*, although having caught eleven and at least three more than any other team, was only one or two ahead of the field due to the points system.

The other boats, from what we'd heard on the radio had had, like us, their share of bad luck and some having had enough chances to be well ahead but doubles and trebles on 15 kilo in difficult conditions was always going to be a big test for crews and anglers alike.

Also there was the nasty rumour that the reasonable weather of the

"we had caught nineteen marlin, six yellowfin tuna and a mako shark. Team Primetime had amassed a winning 10200 points."

last two days could suddenly be changed by the arrival of Cyclone Ivy that was doing its best to pay us a visit after it had finished setting about Vanuatu.

If the weather was going to intervene then what happened in the interim could well decide the outcome.

After our late single fish we were well in the hunt; tomorrow had got to be a real good day.

And it was. After a shaky start it was a bloody good day.

It was definitely a shaky start. The early bite I left to James but he seemed to have picked up the problem that had beset me in previous days. What looked like a good hook-up, followed by a 200–300 metre run as the rest of the gear was cleared, ended in a slack line once the boat was stopped and we were about to go and collect the fish. That had happened to me four times on the trot two days before and it leaves you wondering what on earth you'd done wrong. A combination of things such as light drags, light and low diameter 15 kilo line and large hooks could all make it difficult to set the hook but a lot of fish were wiping with their bills and collecting the leader in front of the lure making it impossible for a clean hook-up. As a result I had begun to push the drag up hard on the strike so as to either get the hook in straight away or not at all, saving time all round if the fish dropped it quickly and negating the need for the rest of the gear to be cleared and loads of fruitless winding. It had definitely got me one fish that was hooked on the face and later would get me another two where the hook was locked over the bill with only the barb holding it in place.

Just before nine am we were on a double of yellowfin tuna. James failed to stay stuck to a marlin soon thereafter and depressed and confused he decided to stand down and let me take the next few chances. He'd had a really good run but it happens to us all sometimes, it's just not your time of the day. So when the next marlin appeared, as James was studying yet again what prizes he was hoping to win, it was me that quickly pushed the drag beyond the strike mark to get the hook buried somewhere. Then, as before taking off, I eased the drag back some and with the captain deciding not to wait for a double, the gear was cleared and we were quickly after my fish to get it tagged and away before it really woke up.

The hook was lodged in the bill but not even up to the barb and Sean got the tag in not long before the hook pulled out and Mike was left holding the slack leader; we were lucky.

"Have I redeemed myself?" Sean was cocky.

"I guess so. Like that fish, you're off the hook."

We were not as lucky with the next marlin.

As we were backing up and I was collecting line as fast as the little reel would allow, it all went slack and I reeled in an empty line.

Empty of everything.

Hook, lure, leader, swivel, wind-on and maybe fifty metres of 15 kilo line, all gone. Either another fish had cut the line or it had gone through a bait school, either way yet another hot lure was lost and another thirty minutes of re-rigging was required.

The radio had been throbbing with the action from the Middlesex Bank but as with us, a lot of chances had gone begging. Broken lines, lost lures and lost fish, it was a familiar tale, nevertheless our competition were still finding the odd one to keep the pressure on. However, after lunch, we found our form and sprinted away from the pack.

As usual it could have been more but I got two in the afternoon before another strange happening cost us a fish and James decided he was ready to return to the fray after a sulk and a nap.

The strange thing was this. A marlin ate the lure just after it had bounced on a swell; the main line had sprung back and momentarily caught on the rigger clip at precisely the same instant. The result was a broken line just below the loop in the clip and another lost hot lure. I was surprised the captain took it so well and the deckhands had to re-rig the whole deal again. And just in time because as soon as we were completely back in action again we were bit again.

James brushed me aside as I was singing "three nil, three nil, three nil, three nil, three nil, three nil, three nil" and collected his first marlin of the day at nearly half past five in the evening.

The bait was "up" and as Mike says, "the marlin were on the chew."

At six o'clock we were on a double and mine for once stayed on and at 120 kilos was the biggest we'd caught. James' fish escaped early on.

4–1, it was like playing Tottenham.

At seven, with the bite in full swing James insisted on taking the next one that appeared. He got it to the boat pretty quickly and we even got the tag in but as soon as some extra weight was applied to the leader the marlin bolted. After that it was a real stubborn so and so. With the fish continually dogging down and with only 15 kilo gear it was hard for

James to get the 110 kilo fish up and keep it up, every time the leader was collected the marlin would bolt again.

It was feeling the hook and the time dragged on.

Bite time was evaporating, fish were being caught elsewhere and the captain was visibly distressed. His muttering turned to frustration, frustration turned to anger, anger to despair. The fish took us nearly two miles before finally tiring enough to be leadered and after going down twenty times and James had brought it up twenty one.

We steamed back into the bite zone, it was nearly dark, we recommenced fishing but it was all over for the day.

Still six fish, six more which had stretched our team's lead; both James and I had caught eight marlin each. James' points total had reached 4600 and mine 4000.

I had him in my sights now.

He was looking nervous.

"Dad?"

"Yup, what's up J'Bud?"

"You still need two more to beat me on points you know?"

"Yeah, so?"

He was thinking. No not so much thinking as plotting. The wheels were grinding, I could hear them.

"I'll tell you what Jamesy. We'll take it in turns tomorrow, chance by chance, no matter what."

"OK I go first."

"Hold on you just got the last one and spent over an hour on it costing us more fish in the process."

"Yes but that won't happen again." He seemed sure.

"OK J'Bud, you get the first go in the morning, as long as you're ready."

"What do you mean, ready?"

"You know, up and about, teeth brushed, ablutions completed. Ready."

"You will wake me up, won't you?"

"Well! If I'm up and about first and you're still getting dressed..."

"I'll get ready now. I'll sleep in my clothes. I'll even keep the belt for the gimbal harness on."

And he did.

At 0730 shortly after lures in James pushed the drag up on the first marlin of the day and it could have been the same fish from the night before.

We none of us could believe it.

This one took us nearly two miles in slightly less time but employed the same tactics.

The captain was not amused.

By the time it was done and dusted James was considering going back to bed.

Nearly another hour of prime bite time lost but at least like the one before we had got it.

We were on the board and on the move.

The morning dragged on with few chances but the news from the weatherman was the worst.

Cyclone Ivy was on her way.

We had just over 24 hours to get home before it arrived and in the morning it would be 35 rising 45 knots and maybe from the east or southeast.

The worst possible.

The radio was abuzz with nervous chatter.

Some boats were getting out immediately; *Striker*, our nearest rival was going mid-afternoon. Two others, *Harlequin* who had already tagged two or three this morning and *Independence*, another on our tails, were talking about sticking around for one more night.

In that case we would be staying too.

It was "Last man standing" stuff. Who would blink first?

The captain was making calculations; I knew it wouldn't be him.

He reckoned that if any of the others got five or six more fish we could lose our lead.

Even though it was highly unlikely, I knew we wouldn't be going anywhere until the others cleared out.

"the fish, seemingly surprised at such an outrage, burst out of the water"

It could well be a long and uncomfortable day.

It certainly would be tomorrow, regardless.

At half past one I got another yellowfin tuna.

"My turn next," said James.

"Hold on, it wasn't a marlin."

"No matter, that was your chance gone."

"But you are three ahead now."

"So?"

"Yeah, so?"

"So! Looks like I'm going to win then."

As though the fish knew the game was up, it went very quiet.

At half past three a fish appeared on the long corner. James rushed forward and hovered over the reel.

I went to the short rigger and watched the fish swaying about and across the prop wash.

What was it going to do?

Was there a second fish?

There was shouting from the flybridge, the deck came alive and a marlin ate my lure.

The rigger popped, the drop back fell to the surface of the water, the line came up tight and the reel zipped. I pushed the drag up above strike and set the hook into something.

I looked across to my right to see James winding his lure back up to the surface, it had been hit but nothing had taken hold. He got it back into position, eased back the drag and waited with his fingers on the spool for the fish to come back.

A dorsal popped up again. The fish lined itself up and poured in, bill wagging and mouth open. James fed it the lure, the fish turned, the line zipped for a second or so and stopped.

James wound back again and waited.

This time the fish did not come back straightaway and the captain called "time out".

"OK get the gear in, let's get the one we've hooked-up."

It only took a further five minutes to fight mine to the boat and tagged.

The point of the hook was in the bill but not up to the barb.

On the leader the fish made a big effort to escape but only succeeded in pulling the hook right through its bill making it totally secure. With full weight on the leader, the fish settled down, was collected, unhooked and released.

The captain called in the fish straight away to the recorders on the other end of the radio, he also called in the one from early in the morning and the one from late the night before; one we had caught after the previous evening round-up.

It may be that these three fish finally nailed down the lid on the coffin, because even though there were still three or four boats fishing over on the Middlesex Bank, the radio went very quiet. It seemed like we had finally beaten them into submission but we carried on fishing to the bitter end.

By the time the next weather forecast came early in the evening, we had begun to work our way down the King Bank.

The forecast was worse.

Nobody would be staying; it was time to get out.

"Not until *Harlequin* has gone!" The captain was adamant.

"It's your call John, but don't let's spoil a good trip by getting beaten up on the way back."

We carried on fishing until dark when as usual we got another shot but the fish jumped off after a few minutes.

"You won't believe it but we are only in thirty eight metres of water! I was cutting across a corner of the Bank; I have never been in this spot before, ever. It's not even marked on the charts as coming up this shallow. Damn shame it didn't stick!" The captain puffed out his cheeks.

It was time.

"OK the others are on their way to North Cape; *Striker* is running all the way to Whangaroa, we're the last to leave. Pull the gear, tie it all down. The Trough could get a bit messy."

It may have been, I don't know, I was asleep. I woke up when the anchor went down about one in the morning. We had run around the top and were under the North Cape Light. We were alone.

No one was in a hurry to get up in the morning but we crept out into a rising sea at eight o'clock and headed out to the Garden Patch.

It was rising 35 knots and the lures went out.

As the news filtered through on the radio it seemed everyone else had run back as far as they could, some to Whangaroa, some to Houhoura and most had only just got their anchors down. With this sea and the rising wind the ones in Houhoura wouldn't get out again in a hurry.

There were two days left in the Tournament but tomorrow was definitely a no go.

Would anyone other than us brave the weather and give it a try today?

With swells breaking over the flybridge I stuck it out and watched the lures as best I could. James had sensibly given up but if the captain was still fishing then so was I.

The wind was gusting to 60 knots on the west coast and *Striker* was leaving Whangaroa and going out for a look.

I gritted my teeth, the captain just grinned and lit another cigarette.

Fifteen minutes later *Striker* was going back in.

The towel had been thrown in.

We'd done it.

Not official of course for a day or so but if we weren't fishing then nobody would be fishing.

After edging out to make an angle we turned and set course for home with the sea on the port beam and still finding the occasional wave that broke over the deck and would have washed away anyone standing there, or drowned a foolish fisherman strapped in the fighting chair.

So we had caught nineteen marlin, six yellowfin tuna and a mako shark.

Team *Primetime* had amassed a winning 10200 points, 5200 by James and 4400 by me.

James had not only won the Junior Tag and Release Striped Marlin title but the overall Champion Tag and Release Striped Marlin title too. He'd even beaten me on numbers because he'd caught the last of his nine fish first. He cleaned up all the top prizes.

It was left to me to collect the minor honour of Tag and Release Tuna Champion.

Somehow, it did not feel quite the same.

Unfinished Business

Fifty years ago, if you wanted to catch a big broadbill swordfish on rod and line and when I say "big" I mean over six hundred pounds, there were only two destinations, both on the west coast of South America. They were Iquique, Chile and Cabo Blanco, Peru.

Chile figured again briefly in the late 1980s with two six-hundred pounders and the Atlantic Ocean's biggest ever swordfish of nearly 613lb was landed during the South Florida heydays of the late 1970s, but today and for the last few years there has only been one place to go.

Northern New Zealand.

That's not to say that big broadbill aren't still found off the Chilean coast, they certainly are, as the fleet of longliners in the port of Iquique and a trip to the Iquique fish market will amply demonstrate, but unless you want to take your own boat, tackle and crew, out to the Humboldt fishing grounds, (there are no charter boats available) you're stumped.

The Florida six-hundred pounder, caught in 1978 was the first outside Chile or Peru since the 1950s but since 1998 the ten fish over six hundred pounds, including one over eight hundred and two over seven hundred pounds have all been caught in New Zealand waters, and one captain, Captain John Gregory fishing his *Primetime* has found five of them.

After Zane Grey registered the first capture of a New Zealand broadbill in 1926, less than twenty more fish were recorded over the following sixty years. In the few months from March to the end of July 2004, *Primetime* caught twenty up to 704lb, including a fish of 639lb for the well-travelled American fisherman Martin Hirsch.

As well as these two monsters, the biggest of which was unfortunately shark bit on the tail, were two five-hundred pounders and four four-hundred pounders, a record unmatched by any other boat or captain in the world.

From May 2001 until July 2004 Captain John Gregory recorded fifty broadbill swordfish and amazingly, twenty of them were over four hundred pounds.

(The actual figures were nine four-hundred pounders, seven five-hundred pounders, three six-hundred pounders and one seven-hundred pounder.)

There doesn't seem to be a particularly special time to fish for swordfish in New Zealand, most months produce them for the longliners, who each year bring in a few five and six hundred kilo giants, but the New Zealand winter weather prevents all but the most intrepid from venturing out to the various Banks found over one hundred miles from the nearest safe harbour and which offer the best opportunities to the recreational fishermen.

Like most other big game fish species that frequent New Zealand waters, (striped marlin are rarely less than 175–200lb, blue marlin rarely less than 450–500lb, mako sharks rarely less than 250–350lb) the broadbill are well above the size found elsewhere. For example, whereas I have read that the average size of broadbill caught in the rest of the world may well be less than 100lb, a fish that small would be a rare sight indeed in New Zealand. 250lb would be considered quite small in a country where 400lb plus fish are the norm and 500lb plus are to be expected. That's not to say that once encountered they just roll over and jump in the boat, a lot of big fish get the better of their pursuers, and a lot of pursuers don't come back for another go after being beaten up for ten hours in the dark by a creature that won't come quietly until it is just about dead.

So, when the IGFA opened up a raft of new record categories for Junior and Small Fry anglers, including those for broadbill swordfish, my 14-year-old son James set his sights on having a crack at a big sword.

With *Primetime* booked out until the middle of June it seemed wise to wait until the boat's season had ended and we would have the flexibility of being able to pick a window when the weather looked to be most favourable for an extended, six to eight day, stay away from our home port of Whangaroa; the self proclaimed "Jewel of the North".

The problem would be that the regular *Primetime* crew was looking to depart to fresh pastures after a hard but fruitful season and I would have to press-gang a few friends from their normal activities to fill the vacated spaces on the deck and in the galley.

Not a problem you would think but putting together a team at very short notice and one that passed the exacting scrutiny of our erstwhile skipper, was a challenge to say the very least.

"What about so-and-so?" I would say.

"No! I'm not having anyone from the competition on my boat," would be the response.

"Well, what about?"

"He couldn't go a day without a drink let alone a week."

"And?"

"He falls asleep at the slightest opportunity. We'll be doing watches all through the night. I can't stay awake for a whole week. And don't mention whatisname, he wants to see dry land and falls apart if it's blowing more than 25 knots."

"Well, who do you suggest? And you can forget 'the poisoned dwarf'."

"Can't you get your mate Steve to come away?"

"I'll try but I know he's busy working and then there's his new baby. I'll try Johnno too, although he's hard at it on his new boat and he'll need some notice in order to drop everything and come up from Tauranga."

"Well we need one of them and if we can't get away soon we'll need two because love-lorn Mike has got all smitten and nesty and will be out of here and down to Wellington by the end of the month." The captain sighed and shook his head.

"Why can't deckhands be six foot eunuchs, instead of pigmies with their brains in their trousers?" I said, not exactly making him feel better.

"Tell me about it!"

"Well, I'll do my best."

"OK, we're away now for our last trip and are due back on the 15th, so try and get someone for the 17th for a week."

As suspected Johnno was tied up on his boat but would be free later on maybe. Steve was busy but keen and could be available for the 19th, weather and work permitting.

It was now the 13th, the boat would still be away up North and out of cell phone range but I called to leave the message that I'd made some progress.

I was surprised when Captain John answered the phone.

"Hey John, where the hell are you?"

"We're coming down the coast, the charter pulled the plug two days early. We're coming home."

"Problems?"

"I'd say not, we've got three swords on the deck!"

"Shoot!"

"Yup, there's fish there at the moment John, when can you be ready to leave? The weather's going to stay good for a few more days yet."

"Call me tonight when you get home, we'll see then." I needed time to think.

How the heck was I going to pull this off?

James would have to bunk off school, could Steve do the same?

With some flowery embellishment I explained to Steve how well they had done and how the fish were queuing up to get caught.

"Yeah Steve, six fish hooked, three on the deck, piece of cake. If they can do it, so can we. You, James and me; one each. What d'ya say?"

I held my breath and crossed my fingers.

"When would we have to leave?"

"Day after tomorrow maybe, perhaps in the evening? I'll talk to John tonight and let you know."

"And the weather's OK?"

"Yup."

"Ok, I'm in."

"Good man!"

When Captain John called that night I told him about Steve being ready in two days time.

"But we could leave tomorrow."

"Eh?"

"Yeah. I'm fuelled up and we've got baits left over. We can always get more in the morning."

"John, I don't know. We can't go without Steve."

"No, that's right,"

"Let's talk again in the morning." I just couldn't see how it could all fit together so quickly; it was surely better to wait until all parties were available and ready.

But in the morning after James had left for school, a spanner was thrown in the works.

"There's a front coming, if we don't get away today we'll lose the window and who knows when the weather will come right again?" The captain had got the updated weather forecast and a series of lows had popped up off south western Australia and would be marching across the Tasman by the end of the week.

It would be down to Steve.

I got him just before he left for work.

"We're going this evening, weather's forced our hand."

"But?"

There was a pause.

"I'll let you know in a couple of hours."

When I got back to the captain it was agreed that we'd prepare to go regardless. It would be a hectic day; there was much to do.

But by the time James returned from school our bags were packed and gear prepared. Bait and ice had been organised, Steve had dropped everything and was on his way and the stores were being loaded on board the boat.

By six o'clock the fuel bladder was filled and strapped to the port side of the cockpit, by seven we were all onboard and a few minutes later *Primetime* was eased out of it's berth and quietly made it's way up the harbour.

It was cold and misty but calm and at a steady eighteen knots we ran up the coast to North Cape, eased back to fourteen and made a beeline for the Three Kings Islands.

I heard the anchor go down in the early hours and put the ear

"Its lower jaw had been deformed and cut deeply by old fishing line but it had all healed over perfectly."

plugs in to blot out the sound of the tide slapping on the chines and Mike's snoring.

In the morning we made our way to the Middlesex Bank and a spot of wintertime "chuck it and chance it" marlin fishing. We did actually raise three fish during the day but they were half-hearted efforts and even though the lures got whacked a couple of times, nothing stuck.

As the day wore on we worked our way west to the broadbill grounds and the main event.

All that had passed before was just a precursor to the moment when we could begin the real fishing.

There's nothing quite like fishing for unseen monsters, the greater one's imagination the more riveting it becomes and slow trolling a single squid bait in the darkness is designed to get it stirring.

The sun set at six o'clock and at six fifteen the skirted squid was lowered over the stern. A couple of metres or so up the trace two glowing light sticks were attached with elastic bands. The bait was allowed to run back twenty metres or so before the Dacron loop whipped to the main line was attached to the downrigger weight. With the green glow from the light sticks plainly evident behind us, the weight was also lowered over the stern and the meter on the downrigger clicked off the depth as the weight quickly sank out of sight taking the glowing lights down with it. The glow faded and eventually disappeared. The weight was stopped at about one hundred and sixty feet and with the downrigger sited on the port corner; more line was stripped off the reel to create the first drop-back down in the water. The main line was then connected by elastic bands to a release clip on the starboard corner. The release clip being on the end of a short two-foot lanyard to which a glowing light stick was attached.

Our "bite indicator."

The rod was then placed in a rod holder in the port side covering board and more line was stripped off to create a second, u-shaped, drop-back on the surface.

When the fish hit the bait with its sword the downrigger would be tripped and the sub surface drop-back would allow the bait to sink freely and hopefully, naturally. When the fish came back to eat, if it hadn't already done so, and take up the slack line, the release clip would pop, our light stick "bite indicator" would alert us to the take and we would be in business.

With trolling valves on the motors we could tow as slow as one and a half knots easily and be able to stop quickly once a bite occurred.

It would then be a case of waiting.

Back in the 1930s and '40s when the Lerners and the Farringtons were at the height of their success with broadbill in Chile and Peru, they would have coils of line looped on the deck. When the fish hit the bait the coils were tossed overboard and the strike wouldn't take place until at least all the slack was taken up and the line came tight. Farrington reckoned at times it might be ten to fifteen minutes before he would have the boat driven off and hopefully set the hook.

"We've got company, John." The skipper called down to me. "There's five or six good marks on the sounder around this bait school."

He'd seen it many times before. Ten minutes earlier there had been nothing showing but as the bait appeared, having come in from beyond the drop off onto the bank nearly three hundred metres below us, the big predatory marks had just as mysteriously turned up too.

The orange light from the sunken sun was still on the horizon, the single bait had been out for fifteen minutes and as I sat on the stairs leading up to the bridge, the captain said evenly, "I think we've been bit."

He'd seen the line from the downrigger suddenly take up a different angle.

As I moved down onto the deck the slight green glow reappeared back behind the boat and was getting more apparent all the time.

The downrigger had tripped. Was it a bite?

With both engines out of gear the boat gently eased ahead with the residual forward motion. As Mike wound up the downrigger weight, the green glow edged out towards the port, the release clip popped and with an audible crack, the "bite indicator" sprang up before falling back and hitting the stern.

I went to the rod, lifted it out of the holder, took it to the fighting chair, buckled the reel up to the harness and sat back and waited.

The glow from the light sticks was still evident but it seemed the light was no longer moving.

"Come on fish, come back. Come back fish and eat it!" Like Hemingway's Santiago I willed the fish to return and waited.

We all waited.

Everyone else was now on deck. James, who had decided not to take

"By the time we got back to Whangaroa at one in the afternoon for the weigh-in of the fish, which incidentally went close to 240 kilos"

the first fish so he could see what he was in for, was standing behind me and steering the chair so that the rod was pointing at the direction the line was going. Steve and Mike were watching the green glow, which at last, began to move ahead and unfortunately, up our port side. The captain was forced to go ahead too. Slowly at first and then faster as the green glow sped up and then shot in towards us passing just astern before quickly disappearing out on the starboard.

I sat transfixed in the chair. Even with all this activity, not one inch of line had left the reel.

And nor did it.

I wound the reel slowly and collected the slack line before feeling only the slight weight of the bait and as the light sticks' glow got closer to the boat it was obvious to all that the fish had gone.

We all fell on the bait as it came aboard.

It was totally unmarked.

There was a slight scuff on the leader near the disarranged light sticks but no other clue as to what had happened.

"Must've whacked the light sticks and got the line caught up somewhere," was the captain's judgement. "It knew something was wrong, that's why it charged the boat."

"Did it?" I was surprised.

"Oh yeah! I had to put the hammers down to get ahead when it shot in like that. It was right on us. Never mind I'll run back to the bait and we'll try again."

Once back in position the bait was presented as before and all eyes remained glued to the light stick indicator that rose and swayed with the swell.

The wind began to freshen and a solid band of rain appeared on the radar some four miles out and sweeping our way. With all light from the sun now gone and no moon, it was dark and cold and getting colder. Whilst the captain was still sporting his shorts I was robed in three layers, the inner being thermal and the outer being waterproof.

Replacements and extras were laid out in my cabin. Replacements for the ones that would be drenched in perspiration if I had to go to work for an extended period and extras for the hours before dawn when the temperature would fall even more.

We watched and waited and the captain fought with the wind and the current to keep the boat on course at such a slow speed.

He still, however, saw the first sign of a bite before anyone else.

"The light stick's up!"

Before I had time to look back, I heard the crack as the band in the release clip sprang out, the drop back disappeared rapidly, the line came up tight and the reel began a slow to moderate zip.

Mike, as before, wound up the downrigger weight, I took the rod to the chair and we all took up our positions.

The line trickled off intermittently as the seconds passed, but with my fingers gently on the line, I could feel the weight of the fish.

"He's still there," I said.

"He sure is!" said Steve, as the fish burst out about fifty metres behind us and thrashed on the surface; the white water clearly evident in the dark. "It's only about fifty kilos!"

There was an exclamation from the bridge and the boat powered forward as the glow from the light sticks hurtled in towards us.

"It's bigger than that!" yelled the captain, hard at work at the helm.

I pushed up the drag and wound until the rod arched over and the reel complained briefly before it all went slack and I thought the fish was off.

We all thought it was off.

I wound and wound before seeing the glow again much closer and the boat surged forward yet even faster.

"The bastard's charging us!" yelled the skipper.

I still wound and wound until there couldn't have been more than twenty metres of line out and the fish came to the surface right behind the boat, waving its sword and crashing around.

"It's wrapped up, it's wrapped up!" yelled Mike. "The leader's coming off its tail!"

We continued to go ahead until we were really tight to the fish and I worked it as hard as I could. The fish stayed on the surface and beat the surface with its tail as it got the message that it was in trouble and tried to get away from us. It began to make some headway and we backed up and gave chase, slaloming from side to side as the fish dived first one way and then the other with its dorsal and tail slicing through the swells.

For nearly five minutes it took us for a walk with the leader visible but out of reach until the fish suddenly sounded and we had to put the brakes on and do an emergency stop.

The diesel smoke wafted around me and the water on the deck began to drain out of the scuppers.

One of the captain's marlin chasing tricks is to have one engine just in forward gear as we pour backwards on the other. This means a quick change of direction is possible without the frustrating delay of the gearbox shifting from one way to the other. He'd never run over a hooked fish but had come mighty close on occasions and broadbill could alter course even quicker than marlin.

With the fish going down we could get ourselves reorganised and draw a breath.

"Man, did you see that sucker take a shot at us?" The excited sparkle in Mike's eyes lit the darkness.

"It's a bloody good fish, did you see how fat it was?" Steve joined in the chorus of approval.

"What happened to fifty kilos, then Steve?" Captain John got the barb in before the rest of us could respond.

"Yeah. Well. Mmm." Steve's voice faded into an embarrassed silence.

The deck lights were put on and the gaffs were coming out when we were hit by a squall.

The wind lashed the rain onto my waterproof hood and back and I knew that, other than James who would dutifully man his post behind the chair, I would be alone on the deck.

The rain beat the sea to foam and the boat rocked and swept sideways with the wind.

The fish eased its run and I was able to get to work. Knowing that the fish was probably wrapped I had nothing to lose by piling on the pressure. With me hauling on its tail it couldn't swim as effectively as it might and if, as it appeared likely, it had wraps around the body or gills, I could have a serious advantage.

I needed one in the conditions, because in order to keep the angle on the fish straight behind, the captain had to swing the stern into the wind. The rain greeted me by stinging my hands and face and eventually penetrated a gap, ran down the back of my neck in a cold stream and worked out a route to my crevice.

With all such inconveniences banished from my thoughts I pumped the fish back up. Once or twice it fought back momentarily and I lost some line but the time came when I knew it was over bar the shouting.

The line was coming steadily; I had never had more than one hundred and fifty metres out anyway and had not been down to the Dacron backing. There was no movement from the fish, not even a tail wag. It was heavy but on the move and I continued to work as the ironmongery clanked on the deck.

The rain stopped, the wind abated and the Dacron loop appeared and I duly wound it on. It was followed, not long after by the double line and Mike eased on the leader as I continued to wind.

Out the fish came tail first and rolled on the surface. Steve placed the big gaff over its back and leaned back. The fish didn't flicker.

Mike got the second gaff into the anal fin area and the captain threw tuna bombs to ward off the sharks.

I got out of the harness and the chair and slipped open the fish door as the fish was led around towards it. James, using a small fixed gaff, collected the sword and lifted it until I could grab it and guide it through the opening. It was then a case of waiting for a swell and all heaving together.

"OK. One, two. Go!" We all fell back as the fish slipped through the door and a swell washed it up the deck. I ran and closed the door quickly and our eyes fell on the fish.

It was so fat and full it rolled on the deck like a stuck pig.

"Look how fat it is!" The captain came down and grasped my hand and shook it repeatedly. "Just over thirty minutes, what a job. Look how fat it is!" he said again, shaking my hand even more.

"Two fifty all day." Mike propounded, not expecting anyone to disagree and getting to work with the tape measure.

The still-baited hook hung limply along the big broadbill's flank. The leader was loosely looped around its body a couple of turns and there was one tighter loop around the root of its tail. Other than a few old cookie cutter shark scars the fish was clean and it glistened in the deck lights. Its lower jaw had been deformed and cut deeply by old fishing line but it had all healed over perfectly. In the corner of its mouth was a smallish galvanised offset circle hook that had almost corroded through at the place on the bend where it had been touching the fish.

"Will you look at that?" said the captain.

"It certainly didn't affect it feeding, this fish is stuffed to the gills," said Steve, prodding the hard gut as the fish rolled again. "It's as round as a bloody barrel."

"Well James, you ready for one now?" I turned to my son and clapped him on the shoulder.

"No worries, bro," he stated confidently, defying the expensive English boarding school education he'd enjoyed before reaching Antipodean shores.

"Hey. 'Yes Dad', will suffice, sunbeam, if you don't mind."

After cleaning up and fitting a new leader as we ran back to start again, James got himself ready by altering the footrest on the fighting chair and adjusting the harness, then we both went inside to change into dry clothes.

In the meantime, a new bait was lowered to its fate, the bite indicator glowed gleefully and my prize, covered in bags of salt ice, was zipped up in the big fish bag and secured to the port side of the cockpit.

When the release clip popped again some hours later the fish gave itself away almost immediately by leaping clear of the water and doing a backwards somersault. Mike was at the helm and John had just retired to his cabin for a bit of shuteye.

"You've got yourself a mako, James!" I said as I wound up the downrigger weight.

James stood by the rod as the mako came out again about twenty metres closer and crashed back with a mighty splash.

"It's a biggie," I said, as I moved to the back of the chair.

James was still by the rod in the port corner and had not yet moved when the fish came out again right behind us and Mike moved the boat steadily ahead.

I knew what was about to

"it was lean and battle-scarred and generally pretty scruffy looking but James hugged it like a long lost pet"

happen but had no time to say a word before the big shark launched itself out of the sea about ten feet from where James was standing and climbed high into the air, whilst fixing us with it's black eye, before it tumbled backwards and smashed seaward again.

Mike put the power on and span the boat as the fish tried to go up the portside and turn under the hull.

"Jesus, that was close. How the hell it didn't take out the port rigger, I'll never know." Mike was getting the boat away as fast as he could and I ushered James into the chair and he got to work.

"It's always the same, the minute I get my head down, Mike finds a damn shark." The captain stumbled onto the deck, hopping on one leg and trying to find a hole in his trousers to insert the other.

"Don't show it any respect James, Just give it the treatment." I knew what makos were like and with a mono leader it was fifty-fifty anyway that it would bite through the line.

Sure enough ten minutes of bullying and James had the fish on the leader and Steve punched home the tag before the fish was cut away.

It wasn't a sword but James was rapt. It was his first mako shark and at an estimated 240 kilos it was a real good one.

"Why the blazes did you just stand there when it jumped in your face?"

"I couldn't move, I knew what was coming but I just couldn't move," replied James wistfully. "And you know what, Dad?"

"What?"

"They've got real bad breath."

With everything reset, the rigged squid cruising along 40–50 metres down and the captain back in his cabin, we were ready for another bite.

When it came, the slow take and gentle clicking of the reel had us believing we were onto the real thing and the captain was dragged from his cabin and back out into the cold night air.

Like the rest of us he was not overly amused when an angry hundred kilo mako was dragged to the boat and especially not when it climbed up the starboard corner, rolled back its gums and gave us its best tooth-laden snarl.

"Get rid of the damned thing and let's get away from here."

Nobody disagreed with the captain but I was able to confirm the halitosis slur.

A change of position found us, an hour or so later, back shivering on the deck and James harnessed to the rod and sitting watchfully in the chair.

The line trickled off and stopped, trickled off some more and stopped again.

Seconds became minutes and the glow from the light sticks eerily rose to the surface.

We waited but the fish didn't come back.

On retrieval the bait had been slashed almost in two and it hung forlornly on the hook. There was no doubt as to the identity of the culprit.

Again we repeated the process with a fresh bait and sure enough there was a repeat performance with the bait coming back squashed but ultimately ignored.

As dawn approached and the coldest part of the night was upon us, we were bit again but this time by an unseen shark that bit through the leader.

After this, yet another false alarm, the captain gave up trying to sleep and returned to the helm.

We didn't get another bite.

After the sun came up at seven o'clock the marlin lures were dusted off and run out for a wash. At seven thirty we got the news we always dreaded.

Another front had popped up south of Tasmania. In thirty-six hours or so it would be, as Steve so eloquently put it, "blowing its tits off."

The rest of the day was as gloomy as it could get. We would get only half the night in before making the long race home; a journey that could take ten to twelve hours at best and a day at worst. Sure enough there was a good fish on the deck, no complaints about that, but it wasn't the one we were after and if it didn't happen that night, then it was anyone's guess when we could get the weather and a team to get back out.

The day dragged on pointlessly and we took turns to sleep as best we could and get ready for the night.

I agreed with the captain that we should fish to three am at the latest and pray that if we hooked-up at five to, that it wouldn't be a protracted battle.

We needn't have worried because other than an early evening trip to the chair for James and the subsequent recovery of a broadbill-mangled bait, the night was fruitless and not long after three am the towel was thrown in and we took off.

The whole of the return journey was conducted in near flat calm conditions and I awoke an hour after first light as we approached the turn round North Cape.

By the time we got back to Whangaroa at one in the afternoon for the weigh-in of the fish, which incidentally went close to 240 kilos, the wind had begun to puff up and rain threatened.

"It was so fat and full it rolled on the deck like a stuck pig."

On the run down the coast I'd planned with John Gregory the outline of our next attempt that was to take place as soon as I could put it together. Neither Mike, who was straight off to Wellington to get his nether regions attended to, nor poor Steve, who was still awaiting his first crack at a sword, would be available and it would be with a totally different crew. Nevertheless we had "unfinished business" to attend to and James and I couldn't wait to get the job done.

But wait we did.

For days and then weeks the lows poured across the Tasman in a seemingly endless stream. Two or thee days of blow would be followed by one or two of fair before it would blow again.

At first I kept in touch with the captain frequently

but then after a while I tired of looking at the forecasts and stood down.

It was a month after our return when, out of the blue one Saturday morning, I got the call.

"The weather looks good for the next four to five days, John. And it's the same phase of the moon."

"What about a crew?"

"We need two, I'll leave that to you."

"I'll give it some thought and get back to you."

I got onto the Internet and checked the forecasts. I didn't think it looked quite so rosy. It was blowing hard outside and boy it was cold. I looked out across the fields, remembering the frost that was on them when I'd got up, and I made some phone calls.

Johnno was working on his boat down in Tauranga when I got him.

He was keen to take a break from the fibreglassing he'd been struggling with in the frosty weather and could be up north by Monday or Tuesday.

Good.

Next I called another friend and one with whom James had also fished before, both on our own boat and a different charter boat, and also someone who had brought us luck in the past. Brent had boated a record yellowtail kingfish for my daughter Gemma and was driving my boat when we'd got my other son Robbie a record skipjack tuna. He was also, like Steve, quite a character a lot of fun and the sort of guy you wanted by your side when the chips were down. Brent wasn't fishing any more and had been driving a concrete truck for a year or two but I'd guessed that he would jump at the chance to get back to sea for a week and I was right. But boy I was lucky, he'd only just got back from a holiday that had been curtailed, if not for which he'd still be down in Taupo with his partner.

I relayed the news to the captain.

"Very good. When can Johnno get here?"

"Maybe Monday night, Tuesday morning?"

"That's pushing it, the weather will turn again by next weekend. I'd like to get away tomorrow night."

"Tomorrow?" I couldn't believe it. Not again.

"Let me know by the morning, or I'm going diving and won't be back until mid-afternoon."

By Sunday morning not much had changed other than it looked on for Monday night and that ice and stores could be arranged for Monday afternoon. But then, mid-morning, Johnno called to say he was on his way after all and would arrive by eight pm.

I called Brent. No problem, he'd be there too.

I got John Gregory just as he was about to slip over the side with his first bottle and set about the crayfish population outside Whangaroa Harbour.

For him, the rest of the day was a blur.

Stores, livebaits, half a ton of flaked ice… he didn't draw breath. But sure enough by nine pm it and five bodies were all on the boat and ready to run over to the fuel dock to fill up the 500 litre fuel bladder.

That was until the starboard motor cut out and died on us.

With a boat load of captains on board the fault couldn't stay hidden for long and was eventually isolated to a dodgy cell on one of the dedicated starboard motor batteries.

It was not enough of a problem to prevent us from sailing, so with the portside motor batteries and the house batteries switched in for good measure, we got the extra fuel before easing out of the harbour at midnight and sweeping up the coast at a healthy eighteen knots.

We arrived at the Three Kings at dawn and filled up on more live baits, many of which were chased to the boat by some fair-sized yellowtail kingfish. When the live wells were full we switched our attention to the "kingies" and sent a couple of freshly caught, bridle-rigged koheru back into the fray. James and I warmed up on some hard-scrapping forty pounders before we had to start the next leg of the run to the broadie grounds, still some 45 miles or more away and some "unfinished business."

James didn't need any more coaching and until the job was done he would be "in the chair". I was confident he would be up to the task, he was fourteen now and a giant in comparison to the pale eleven-year-old who had gone fifteen rounds and three hours with a 530 pound blue marlin. And, in the darkest moments of the fight (there was always at least one), I'd be right behind him, easing him through his pain.

Well I'd be right behind him.

And I'd try not to moan when he was pumping instead of winding.

Maybe I'd just be quiet.

Well I was that first night; there wasn't much to shout about.

Another sword-slashed bait, early on, for James and then a long cold sojourn until just before dawn, another shark bit through the leader.

So far, in his quest, James had sat down to probably four broadbill bites and had not yet felt the weight of a fish.

Surely his turn would come.

Or was he destined to wait and wait like so many others before him?

I could sense his disquiet and knew that in the past he would have been close to giving up by now and I was almost expecting him, later when we would be alone in our cabin, to suggest that it might be better for me to take over for a while.

No such suggestion came.

He was a more determined character now and even though he'd had to wait a little bit, it wasn't to be for very much longer.

At dawn we ran upwind about fifteen miles and shutdown for the day.

The captain slept and the rest of us dozed in the warm sun and someone tossed a livebait out under a balloon, just in case. The bait swam around all day and around four in the afternoon it was retrieved, unsullied and as fresh as it had been six hours earlier.

The sun went down at six and the captain cruised around until he was happy we were in the right place. The bait was moving up onto the bank and was closely shadowed by a number of promising looking marks.

By six thirty the stage was set.

The rigged squid was down at the required depth above the bait schools, the U-shaped drop back was playing on the surface behind the boat and the light stick "bite indicator" hummed and mesmerised in the starboard corner.

We had just had dinner.

Everyone was outside, either on the deck, sitting on the stairs or up in the flybridge but all eyes were on the bite indicator.

Mine were on it when it sprang up and the release clip snapped open.

I went to the downrigger and wound up the weight.

No glow appeared from the light sticks near the bait and for a nerve-jangling thirty seconds nothing else happened as we drifted slowly ahead.

James stood by the rod and at last the line began to trickle off the reel, with the drag barely above free spool the reel clicked, before pausing and then gently trickling again.

James slipped the rod out of the holder, moved easily to the chair and buckled the clips of the harness bucket he was sitting in to the lugs on the reel. I could see the silhouette of his face against the orange light of the fallen sun on the horizon.

He puffed out his cheeks and chewed his bottom lip as he felt the line with his left hand as it trickled and stopped, trickled and stopped and ran off steadily again for a few metres before stopping again.

With the motors out of gear we drifted with the fish as it carried on its business below, seemingly oblivious to its predicament, and we waited.

Slowly the line trickled off again, so gently it seemed incredible that such an immensely powerful creature could be behaving so delicately, so unhurried and obviously totally without concern.

I edged the chair around to follow the direction the line was taking and before long James was facing to port and the line continued to depart, in fits and starts, from the reel.

"James," the captain called down, "I'm going to gradually manoeuvre the boat around until the fish is behind us, then, when I say, ease the drag up to the strike position and I'll power the boat ahead."

I adjusted the chair as the move progressed and James got the call from above. He pushed the drag up to the pre-set position, I gave the thumbs up and the boat moved forward.

The steady clicking became a roar as the rod gradually heeled over and James was pulled up out of his sitting position. He leaned back comfortably against the weight of the fish as it began to wake up to the twenty-two kilos of drag now set against it. It ran for a short way and as the boat slowed the fish turned and James was able to bounce on the chair and recover some line.

"It's coming back at us!" James wound and collected the line as fast as it would come onto the reel and keeping in touch with the fish until the captain had to run the boat away and wait for the fish to settle down again. James maintained a steady pressure, pumping and winding when he could and gradually drawing us together.

The Dacron loop came onto the reel and the fish, after only ten or fifteen minutes was close to the boat and hadn't yet attempted to sound.

A voice in my head kept saying "shark" but I kept quiet, watched the line and kept the chair straight as James continued to work the fish.

"Not again." I thought. "Please, not again."

The line kept coming, the double line appeared and a dark erect dorsal followed by a sickle-shaped tail scythed through the surface and swept away, causing the reel to scream and forcing James to grab the base of the chair with his right hand.

John had the boat in reverse and taking chase in the blink of an eye and as we careered backwards the swells washed over the transom and sluiced the teak deck.

James collected line when he could and as the double line became evident, the fish dived, forcing the skipper to throw out the anchors.

The fish was going down.

James could have a brief rest, albeit straight legged up in the air, and the line cracked off the reel and steadily disappeared into the depths. We were not over the drop off yet, two or three hundred metres was going to be easier to recover than the two thousand it might become a quarter of a mile away.

But the fish never went down that far.

After less than two hundred metres the fish stopped and James was able to work it slowly back up to around fifty metres, probably close to the depth it had taken the bait, and the war of attrition began in earnest.

"James and I warmed up on some hard scrapping forty pounders"

Ten to fifteen metres won, ten to fifteen metres lost. The Dacron loop would be wound on, only to be pulled off again. Over and over until Johnno advised us that one hour had passed since the initial bite.

"Just keep at it James, it can't do this forever, you're working it really well, just don't let it rest in its comfort zone." As I peered over his shoulder to watch the line on the reel, I saw his right thigh trembling with the effort.

He was feeling it too now.

"Work your way through it son. Keep smooth and focussed. I promise you, you're winning."

As the Dacron loop left the reel for the umpteenth time James plumped back in the chair and I saw him sag noticeably. And the fish led us out over the drop off.

It was one of the dark times.

When the voices come and the doubts creep in and the harness feels uncomfortable, the hands start to hurt and the legs feel like jelly. A time to regroup mentally and stay focussed.

"I know what Steve would say, if he were here," I thought to myself.

But I refrained from yelling.

"Get hard, you pussy!"

Instead I said: "James allow yourself to sit down and give your thighs a rest."

He rolled his right shoulder back and sat down gently.

"Now let the weight of the fish take all the stretch out of the line, push the drag up a bit more if you want, and then when the weight is at its heaviest make short dips with your body and retrieve maybe only a quarter of a turn at a time. Keep doing it as steadily as you can without letting the line get back its elasticity. You'll get the fish started back up that way, you'll see."

He tried and for a good while it was fine until he got his timing a bit wrong when a big swell lifted the boat and the fish started down again, back to its comfort zone.

"Quick, try again, don't let it rest." I urged James back into action.

For a while he whined and complained and I knew how he felt, I'd done the same myself, but I also knew that he would get through it with a bit more encouragement.

"You've got to keep it up, I promise this will beat it, you'll see. Try again."

He tried again with a similar result but this time the fish took back a lot less line and I sensed that this was the chance we needed.

"You've done for him James, reel him up."

When James got to work again there was no fight back from the fish and the rod flexed steadily and rhythmically and the line built on the reel inches at a time, then half a turn then a turn until the loop appeared.

"OK James you know that's the tag where the lure gets clipped up in the long rigger when we're marlin fishing, reel in the lure buddy, that's all you have to do, reel in the lure."

The turns were coming faster and James was sweeping the fish up easily and it burst through the surface just behind us and wallowed lifelessly.

Johnno collected the leader and eased the fish to the boat, Brent placed the first gaff over its back and I completed the job with the other by the anal fin and we led it to the now open door.

With the tuna bombs going off all around it I hooked-up the sword and we struggled to haul the whole lot through the door.

James hopped out of the chair to assist and his prize reluctantly slid into the cockpit to a great cheer.

He'd done it!

It wasn't the prettiest swordfish you'd ever see, it was lean and battle-scarred and generally pretty scruffy looking but James hugged it like a long lost pet and we all slapped him on the back until he was sore.

"Very good," said the captain as he came down to join the throng. "Very good, just the way I like 'em." He was referring to the hook-up; the bait was barely visible and right down the broadbill's throat. "That wasn't coming off!"

Under the tape measure the fish proved to be a similar size to the one we'd boated a month before, in that it was the same length but the girth was less and didn't carry too far towards the tail.

The captain called it one twenty which I thought a bit mean and suggested one forty to one fifty kilos.

"I reckon the length will save it, John, it's got the dimensions of a one ninety."

"It won't go that, but never mind, it's a world record! Well done James!"

James flushed up a trifle but with pride not embarrassment and we all wallowed shamelessly in the light of our success.

Business was no longer "unfinished" but we were not quite done yet.

"You ready for another one James, maybe a bit bigger?"

"Not tonight Dad, not tonight, I hurt all over."

"Yes I know but you did the right thing, you set yourself against the fish and did what you had to do. It will be easier next time."

"OK, but not tonight,"

I was sitting on the stairs leading up to the bridge and James had gone inside for a set of dry clothes and a rest. It was less than an hour since James' fish had been iced and bagged up and a fresh bait had gone over the stern.

"Hey John, look at this on the sounder, that's a broadbill mark, I know

---

Left: "With the official photographs taken and the IGFA paperwork completed and signed off, for James, business was finally 'finished.'" Right: "I just gotta find a crew."

it. Plain as day, just look at that." The captain summoned to me.

As I rose and turned to make my way up to the bridge to join him, I heard the crack as the elastic band snapped out of the release clip and almost as quickly the drop back was taken up and the line ran slowly off the reel.

Brent was on the deck having a quiet smoke. He went to the downrigger and I took the rod to the chair and sat down. The call to battle stations had brought the other two into the cockpit and James steered the chair as I got organised.

The line stopped running out and I felt the line and tried to judge if there was any weight at the other end. I couldn't tell.

What was going on down there?

"Light stick's up!" advised the captain.

"Is it on the move?" I called back.

"Can't tell," came the reply.

So we waited.

Every now and then the reel would click and I would lose a foot or so of line but was it the fish or was it the action of the swell on the boat?

I tried to imagine what was going on.

Was that a tap, tap?

Did the fish have the bait?

Was it circling around, trying to find it again?

The minutes passed and I was tempted to reel in but I continued as before and we waited some more.

Fully eleven minutes had passed when the captain exclaimed. "Get the drag up quick!"

The motors growled and we surged forward taking up the slack line. The glow from the light sticks was approaching rapidly and as the line came up tight a good sized broadbill, judging by the distance between its dorsal and tail, tore across the surface like a blue marlin, kiting out to my left and going away. We shot off after it and I wound as fast as I could. Just like a good striped marlin "wham bam thank you ma'm" chase we backed down on the hounding fish.

"If the fish stays up like this, we could get an early shot," advised the skipper.

The leader was out and swerving all over the place with us in hot pursuit.

As we began to get on top of it the fish stopped and thrashed on the surface, I kept winding and Johnno grabbed the leader. Just seconds before the moment was right for either a tag or a gaff shot the fish swept out by the starboard corner and Johnno held on bravely. We could have tagged it right then but we just weren't ready for such an early shot and the leader sprang back in Johnno's hands and the moment and the fish were gone.

"That was a real good fish!" exclaimed the captain, the excitement of the chase still in his voice.

"That was bigger than the one you got last time and it was just as deep. That was over two fifty, I tell you!"

"Well it was fun, that's for sure! Imagine that, a sword inside five minutes!"

Three days later after nothing more than sharks and a couple more mangled baits we were back in Whangaroa and at the weighstation. For once word of our arrival had circulated and a small crowd was waiting to greet us.

James' fish weighed 177.6 kilos, much to the surprise of the captain and it looked all of that as its long frame was hoisted up to the delight of the admiring audience.

With the official photographs taken and the IGFA paperwork completed and signed off, for James, business was finally "finished."

But as I watched him posing proudly with his first sword, my mind drifted back to that night and my own thrilling five minutes and knew that mine was far from being finished.

"I just gotta find a crew."

The Unbreakable Record

Like anglers before me I have become intrigued by the broadbill swordfish, not devoted or even obsessed like some have been but its raw power coupled with the mystery associated with such a deep ocean wanderer make it a fascinating adversary.

The history of rod and reel fishing for broadbill, the associated records and the characters that made it their life's goal, is even more interesting.

William Boschen caught the first broadbill on rod and line in 1913 off Avalon, Catalina Island, Southern California and it weighed 355lb. To a large degree, the capture of this fish marked the start of the most amazing development in tackle design and usage that saw the age-old handline and harpoon techniques banished to the dark ages.

Boschen's guide was George Farnsworth who manoeuvred the two-hooked bait in front of the fish using a kite.

Rod and reel fishing for "big game" (tuna, marlin and swordfish) had started in California in the mid-1890s with the capture of bluefin tuna using tackle previously developed in Florida in the 1880s for tarpon fishing. This tackle, especially the rods and reels, was unsuitable and inadequate and whilst "Tuna George" Farnsworth was developing "kite-fishing" to present a bait away from the boat, Boschen invented the "internal star-drag" reel and the fun began in earnest.

For the first time anglers would be able to use a reel where the handle didn't spin backwards as the fish took line. The age of the "knucklebuster" was over.

Boschen, who would not fish for anything other than tuna, marlin and swordfish, became obsessed with swordfish and it wasn't long before others felt the same.

"To the majority of anglers it may seem unreasonable to place swordfishing in a class by itself — by far the most magnificent sport in the world with rod and reel." So wrote Zane Grey. "Let any fisherman who has nerve see and feel a big swordfish on his line and from that moment he is obsessed."

Selwyn "Kip" Farrington who also figures highly in the broadbill records named his house on Long Island "Finning Out" after the manner in which the broadbill relaxes on the surface in the daytime.

Farrington wrote "No words of mine could ever do justice to the broadbill swordfish as the greatest sporting gamefish of them all."

Ernest Hemingway, who could not quite understand the fuss over broadbill, suggested that Farrington should have named his sons Xiphias and Gladius. Michael Lerner, another of the time and who helped found the IGFA, vowed that only broadbill fishing would persuade him out of retirement.

Even though great admirers of striped marlin, the fish they would often find in the same locations as broadbill, both Lerner and Farrington would not stop to bait a marlin when on the lookout for "finning" broadbill. One time in Chile, Kip passed 22 tailing striped marlin in a single day, Lerner passed 51! Farrington's desire was fuelled by the fact that it took him six years to catch his first swordfish off Montauk, only to wait another four years before catching the next off Chile. His dedication was then soon rewarded as he caught big fish with regularity.

Back in the early days after word of the exploits of the Californian Tuna Club pioneers spread, the legendary Zane Grey arrived at Avalon in 1914, the same year Boschen got his first striped marlin. At the time the great tuna was seen to be the top blue button prize for anglers of The Tuna Club but the seemingly impossible task of baiting and landing the massive broadbill swordfish was fast becoming the most passionately pursued angling sport.

Even though fishing for them with rod and reel started in California, very few weighed over 500lb, even IGFA Hall of Famer Roy "Ted" Naftzger, who it is thought has caught 49 daytime broadbill using Catalina Tuna Club rules, has a largest of 503lb.

It took Zane Grey's first expedition to New Zealand in 1926 where he caught the country's first broadbill of 400lb to alert the world to a new and maybe better fishery and it came as no surprise to him when eminent English angler Huntingdon White-Wickham landed a monster 671lb 9oz fish there in 1928.

The quest for big broadbill led from Avalon and California to Montauk, Long Island on the Atlantic coast and Nova Scotia in Canada, to Chile and Peru in the 1930s to 1950s and briefly to South Florida in the 1970s before it became a mostly forgotten fish. But a rediscovered New Zealand fishery has now taken centre stage. In recent years a lot of big fish have turned up and the belated acceptance of 130lb tackle will see some realistic effort being rewarded before too long.

The 1930s are often quoted as the "Golden Era of Blue-Water fishing", at least by the people who were fishing then. These were the days when the Greys, the Lerners and the Farringtons were exploring and opening up new grounds. Days like those in the 1950s when Farrington, Glassell and their cronies and the Marrons, Allisons and others were cleaning up the marlin and broadbill off the coast of Northern Chile and Cabo Blanco, Peru.

At Cabo Blanco from 1952 to 1958, thirty nine black marlin between 1001lb and 1560lb were weighed in, including 3 x 1500lb, 1 x 1300lb, 6 x 1200lb, and 6 x 1100lb, plus countless fish between 600 and 900lb; hardly surprising the run didn't continue.

It was a similar story with the broadbill.

Even the Avalon Tuna Club had release badges for tuna and marlin but not for broadbill.

"Whoever releases, swordfish?" was the joke of the time.

Not that tuna was faring much better. In and around America the American public had no taste for big game fish and ate very little of it. Once weighed the fish was generally dumped back at sea for the sharks. In fact a good sport at Cat Cay and Bimini in the Bahamas was to dump the massive bluefins and blue marlin out at sea and then shoot the sharks that came to dinner (one of Hemingway's favourite pastimes). The only tuna taken for commercial use was generally minced for cat food and at times the flying boat from Miami couldn't "land" because of the host of tuna corpses floating around near Bimini.

By the 1950s much of the rest of the world had woken up to the goldmine that was the open ocean and some such as Cuba had discovered the potential of night fishing with kerosene lanterns, initially for smaller baitfish but when the big boys turned up around the bait schools, attracted by the light, the writing was on the wall.

By the 1970s the Cubans had their "longliners" off the coast of Miami using floating amber burning kerosene smudge pots to keep track of their lines. It didn't take long for them to notice that most of the broadbill were caught under the light pots.

At the same time Cyanamid, USA was developing chemical light sticks for the Government to be used in dark areas where fire was a possibility and would also work under water. Two and two was soon added and the South Florida broadbill fishery was plundered.

The Atlantic fisheries, like that off California, produced few fish over 500lb and a very few over 600lb, the biggest being 612lb 12oz off South Florida in 1978. (A fish of 646lb has been noted from Massachusetts, USA in 1972 but details are unconfirmed.)

So it was the mighty Pacific and in particular the waters off the west coast of South America where the Humboldt Current moved close inshore that the real monsters were found but unlike the black and blue marlin that have been caught by the hundreds of 1000lb or more, only one broadbill swordfish has ever been caught on rod and line at over 1000lb and amazingly only one over 900lb. In fact the list of big broadbill is very short in comparison to that of marlin, even though huge fish, some close to 2000lb are regularly brought in commercially in the South West Pacific, particularly in New Zealand, only a few are regularly caught recreationally.

The answer may be that very few anglers fish for them nowadays, they have gone out of fashion, even forgotten in some quarters. They certainly have become no easier to land once hooked, regardless of the immense improvement in tackle, especially lines and reels. But it could just be that, as in the past, the quest for the broadbill swordfish was driven by the competition for records and the desire to say that you'd caught one and then, as one-time Avalon Tuna Club President, George Thomas III wrote, "after the first thrill has worn off, be content to leave them more or less alone".

So once Lou Marron, that fateful day in 1953, totally eclipsed Arthur Hall's three week old record broadbill of 937lb with his enormous fish of 1182lb, more than 300lb bigger than the third biggest fish ever caught, the "Unbreakable Record" was established and the fire extinguished.

It will take a man on a mission to beat it.

The Path to the "Unbreakable Record"

1896   Col C.P. Morehous and W. Greer Campbell fishing out of Avalon Harbour both catch bluefin tuna on rod and reel off Catalina Island, Southern California. Morehous is credited with being the first.

1898   The Tuna Club is established at Catalina for rod and reel tuna anglers, founder.
Charles Frederick Holder weighs in a 183lb bluefin tuna at Catalina. By the end of the season 24 Tuna Club members had caught fish over 100lb.

1899   Col. Morehous weighs in a bluefin of 251lb, this is still a Tuna Club record. Morehous put up a cup for any Club member who caught a bigger tuna. It has never been presented. (However a 269lb fish was caught in 1988 using 80lb Dacron line).

1903   The Tuna Club records its first striped marlin, captured by Edward Llewellyn. It weighed 125lb.

1911   J. K. L. Ross of Montreal, Canada catches a massive 630lb bluefin tuna at Saint Annes Bay, Nova Scotia. An incredible 379lb bigger than the Morehous fish. The Tuna Club offer him Honorary Membership.

1913   William Boschen, who introduced fishing for broadbill, weighs at Catalina the first broadbill swordfish to be caught on rod and line at 355lb. It took a kite flown bait, George Farnsworth was the guide. Farnsworth developed "kite-fishing" to present a dead flying fish to tuna up to 200 feet away from his launch the *Mabel F* and its wake. Incredibly, Boschen, who only had one eye, lands 6 broadbill that season.

Six days after Boschen lands the first broadbill, Francis Raybeth catches the second of 160lb.

1914   Zane Grey arrives at Avalon with tuna and tarpon experience from fishing in Florida. Grey hooks a striped marlin but loses it. Boschen, fishing with Farnsworth off San Clemente Island, 36 miles from Catalina, catches his first striped marlin, it was over 300lb.

1915 Grey fights his first broadbill but loses it at the boat after the reel seizes up.

Eight broadbill were hooked by Tuna Club anglers during the season but none were landed. Boschen loses a huge broadbill after an 11 hour battle.

Grey catches his first striped marlin 118lb and goes on to catch others including one of 316lb and also four in one day. "I could not sleep, eat or rest, I was crazy on swordfish", he complained.

Charles Frederick Holder, "the founding father" dies.

1916 Grey loses two more broadbill. The reel seizes again on the first and the hook pulls out with the fish beaten at the boat. The second is fought for over nine hours by both Grey and his regular boatman Captain Danielson before the huge fish is again lost at the boat when the double line snaps after the rod had broken.

"R.C." Zane Grey's brother catches a 304lb striped marlin, the season's biggest. It was his first season at Avalon.

By the end of the season at Catalina still only three anglers had caught broadbill, including Harry Adams with a gut-hooked fish of 377lb. Ralph Bandini another of the Tuna Club faithful and who often fished with Adams, plays an estimated grander broadbill for nearly ten hours before losing it. The fish was only bill wrapped and the coiled up wire leader slipped off as the beaten fish was drawn to the boat. It was Bandini's first taste of broadbill, he finally landed his first eight years later in 1924.

1917 After three years trying Zane Grey catches first broadbill at Catalina 260lb.

Hugo Johnstone raises the broadbill record to 362lb but later that season William Boschen reclaims the title with new record broadbill of 463lb after a relatively short fight of under three hours. Grey claims Boschen's double-hooked rig had hooked it in the heart. The Tuna Club records eight broadbill for the season.

1918 William Boschen, who would never fish for anything but billfish or tuna, dies. He was in his late 60s. Not only celebrated for his fishing he invented the "internal star drag" reel in co-operation with his boatman Farnsworth. The reel was later developed by Julius Vom Hofe and call the B-Ocean. ("B" for Boschen).

Fishing off the remote San Clemente Island, forty miles south of Catalina, "R.C." Grey gets another season's biggest striped marlin 328lb, one of seven he caught in one day, remarkably the other six were released at the boat, Captain Danielson's *Leta D*.

As in 1915, no broadbill are landed by the Tuna Club members.

1919 By the end of the 1919 season at Catalina only five anglers had ever caught broadbill on rod and line. Zane Grey, "R.C." and Captain Danielson take turns to fight a massive broadbill for nearly 12 hours into darkness, before the fish breaks off whilst feeding on flying fish! Captain Dan later reveals that he cut the line after realising the fish was far from beaten.

1920 Grey sighted 86 broadbill, baited 75, had 16 strikes, hooked 12 and caught one, his second and the season's biggest at Catalina at 418lb. Grey fishing with Sid Boerstler on his 38foot *Blue Finn*.

By now eight anglers had caught broadbill. "R.C." Grey gets a new record striped marlin 354lb whilst fishing on Keith Spalding's boat *Goodwill*.

1921 Mrs. Keith Spalding catches a 426lb broadbill, becoming the first woman to do so. Grey suggests she could not have done it without assistance. The furore that follows ends in Grey resigning from The Tuna Club. Grey builds his own boat *The Gladiator*, Boerstler is the captain. The purpose built boat is 53 feet long with a 12 foot beam and carries enough fuel to last three weeks.

1922 No longer restrained by Tuna Club rules and tired of losing big broadbill on 24 thread (max 66lb) linen line, the maximum allowable under Tuna Club regulations, Zane Grey decides to have custom-made rods, reels, lines and hooks for broadbill swordfish. The new reels were capable of holding 1500 feet of 39 thread (approx 117lb) linen line. The old reels usually a maximum of 600 feet. Boschen had lost over 500 big tuna in one season because the 24 thread line couldn't withstand the fish's first run. Farnsworth said they often lost a dozen hooks a day.

Successful Tuna Club member Harry Adams had caught five broadbill in eight years, Grey had caught only two in nine years.

1923 Grey's initiative pays off. At Catalina in 1923 the Greys sight 140 broadbill, bait 94, get 11 strikes, hook seven and catch four. That season Zane Grey catches three broadbill, 262lb, 298lb and 360lb. His brother R.C. gets his first broadbill 400lb and also a striped marlin 324lb. At this time R.C. was the only man to have caught more than one over 300lb. This was his fifth. His fish were 300, 304, 328, 354 and 324lb.

The broadbill record is raised to 474lb. This fish is captured in record time after becoming entangled in the newly introduced, controversial and seemingly unsporting, "airplane wire leader". Airplane wire was three strands of high tensile wire which when unwound to create single strand leaders coiled up like a spring if not kept taught. Andy Martin the future President of the Tuna Club and the man responsible for the introduction of the new leader, lost the top of his finger after an accident whilst fishing with it. He landed a broadbill in six minutes when the fish became entangled in the coiled leader and was sliced through the gills.

1924 The record is raised to 528lb, another "airplane wire leader" fish. Grey fights only one fish all summer a broadbill of

413lb, then goes to Nova Scotia. He catches two giant bluefin tuna, 684lb after a six hour battle and the new record 758lb, beating his soon to be fishing companion Captain Laurie Mitchell's 710 pounder. The local fishermen called them "horse mackerel" and regarded them as pests as they disrupted their herring fishing and destroyed their nets.

While in Nova Scotia Grey buys a three-masted schooner and renames it *The Fisherman*.

1925 In the first expedition of its kind Grey sails *The Fisherman* from Panama's Perlas Islands and fishes Cocos Island, the Galapagos Islands and the Mexican west coast. He catches a record sailfish 135lb and record yellowfin tuna 315lb off Cabo San Lucas.

A new biggest broadbill is weighed at Catalina 571lb. The dreaded "airplane wire leader" does for the fish. Tuna Club light tackle expert James Jump catches three broadbill in ten days, including one of 441lb and all from his own boat, *Ranger*.

1926 Eleven years after Scotsman A. D. Campbell caught the first striped marlin there of 223lb Zane Grey and his party go to New Zealand. As well as many marlin and sharks he catches the first broadbill outside of California. It weighs 400lb and he hooks but loses another.

On returning to Avalon Zane Grey catches a new record broadbill at 582lb after a five and a half hour battle. He and his brother go on to catch ten broadbill that season at Catalina, five each, including a 515lb fish.

1927 The first broadbill is caught in the Atlantic, off Montauk Long Island, New York. It weighed 193lb. The angler is Oliver Cromwell Grinnell, who caught four more over the next two years up to 369lb. Grinnell had been trying for over three years to catch an Atlantic broadbill, and had rigged a specially prepared mackerel dead-bait.

With Zane Grey remaining in the Pacific Islands for the

summer, "R.C." fishes alone on *The Gladiator* and beats "Z.G."'s record with a fish of 588lb off Catalina. "R.C." catches seven broadbill, beating Boschen's record for one season. He caught his seven from twelve strikes, they weighed 347/355/435/452/281/392 and the record 588lb. In the years the Greys fished at Avalon they caught 42 broadbill. 24 for Zane and 18 for R.C.

"R.C." was using airplane wire leaders but none of his fish were entangled.

Avalon Tuna Club member George C. Thomas III fishing with Farnsworth catches a new Tuna Club record broadbill of 573lb on 24 thread (66lb) line.

This was the only other broadbill caught that season at Catalina. Thomas claimed that he did not enjoy broadbill fishing although obsessed by it. "It is too uncertain." It took him five years of constant effort to get his first. "I believe the average Catalina angler wants to land a broadbill simply for the sake of doing it, and after the first thrill has worn off, he is content to leave them more or less alone."

Also in 1927 a Mr Fred Burnham of San Francisco lands New Zealand's second broadbill 453lb.

1928   Eccentric English angler Huntingdon White-Wickham catches a new record broadbill of 671lb 9oz. This fish confirms New Zealand as a big broadbill location. His fish remained the all tackle NZ record until 2001.

White-Wickham who was known to have watches on each wrist and in most of his pockets, often sported a torch strapped to his right shoulder.

James Jump catches two broadbill in one day at Catalina and also a new light tackle (nine thread, approx 26lb) record broadbill of 365lb.

1929   Stan Ellis of Whangaroa catches New Zealand's second biggest broadbill of 568lb.

1930	Oliver Cromwell Grinnell dies after pioneering broadbill fishing in the North Atlantic. He also successfully introduced trolling Japanese feathers for tuna.
1931	Mrs Lillian Grinnell follows her husband and becomes the first lady angler to catch a broadbill in the Atlantic off Montauk, Long Island. It weighed 245lb 8oz.
1933	W.E.S. Tuker catches 619lb broadbill, the first ever caught off Chile, heralding the start of an amazing run of huge broadbill hooked in the soon to be famous Humboldt Current fishing grounds.
1934	George Garey catches two broadbill in one day whilst fishing the newly discovered grounds off Tocopilla, Chile. His fish both weigh circa 490lb.
	W.E.S Tuker one time British Vice Consul catches new record broadbill 837lb 8oz, again off Tocopilla, Chile, after a nine hour 25 minute battle. Tuker also catches two in one day, 445lb and 672lb.
1935	Harlan Major catches the second biggest ever broadbill 674lb off Tocopilla Chile.
1936	Using his own hand-built 14/0 reel George Garey catches a new record broadbill 842lb off Tocopilla, Chile. Before retiring and leaving Chile, Garey caught eleven broadbill including three over 800lb, the only man ever to do so.
1939	W.E.S. Tuker invites the Farringtons, Kip and wife Chisie (Sara) to Chile to fish for broadbill. The Farringtons sight 73, bait 37, get 26 strikes and land four. Tuker is disappointed. Chisie becomes the first female captor of a South American broadbill 584lb. Kip Farrington had only caught one broadbill, four years earlier off Montauk, Long Island, before their trip to Chile. He had been trying for six years.
	Kip Farrington witnessed the weighing of a monster broadbill that was harpooned commercially, it weighed 1565lb.
	Zane Grey who had probably done more than anyone

to promote big-game fishing, particularly for broadbill swordfish, dies suddenly of a coronary thrombosis; he was 67. Grey was at home preparing for his next expedition to Cairns, where he reckoned 1000lb black marlin could be found.

Also this year, an unknown angler, Ted Seeley from New York, using inadequate tackle, catches two black marlin over 700lb at new grounds off Cabo Blanco, Peru. He was fishing from a 60 foot sailboat and used a piano stool as a fighting chair.

In association with the American Museum of Natural History in New York Mike Lerner forms the IGFA; Ernest Hemingway is a Vice President.

IGFA officers were prohibited from holding world records.

1940   The Lerners, Mike and Helen, arrive in Peru. Mike gets two broadbill in one day, including one of 638lb. Helen becomes the first woman to catch a broadbill in both the Atlantic and the Pacific Oceans. She also gets a new record striped marlin 403lb.

Mike Lerner went on to catch 23 broadbill.

W.E.S. Tuker retakes the broadbill record with another Chilean fish of 860lb. Before retiring Tuker caught 19 broadbill off the coast of Chile.

1941   Fishing in Chile, Kip Farrington catches 853lb broadbill, and also two of 617lb on the same day. His wife, Chisie, becomes the first woman to catch two broadbill in one day, 396 and 659lb. The first in only four minutes and the second in only 38 minutes. She catches seven in her lifetime. Clarence Ellis also gets two in one day, huge fish of 741 and 651lb.

A 1500lb broadbill is harpooned off Peru.

1943   Kip Farrington is decorated by the Chilean Government for promoting Chile's offshore big-game fishing.

1949   The IGFA standardise line weights as follows three thread/12lb, six thread/20 lb, nine thread/30lb, 15 thread/50lb, 24 thread/80lb and 39 thread/130lb.

The 54 thread/ 180lb and monster 72 thread lines eventually disappear from the eligible line categories.

1952 Mrs Millie Allison catches 759lb broadbill, Chile. This remains the woman's 130lb (60kg) line record. Her husband Don catches 780lb fish on the same trip.

Alfred Glassell Jr. catches a 758lb broadbill off Chile, one of the 17 he ultimately caught there. The same year Glassell catches off Cabo Blanco, Peru, six broadbill and seven black marlin including two 1000 pounders.

1953 Arthur Hall weighs the first and still the only 900lb broadbill, a fish of 937lb from Iquique, Chile. Only three weeks later and from the same area Louis Marron catches 1182lb broadbill, "The Unbreakable Record ".

Marron's huge fish was hooked in the dorsal, wrapped up in the leader and was amazingly brought to the gaff in less than two hours.

Alfred Glassell, back at Cabo Blanco, Peru, gets his 1560lb black marlin, another "unbreakable record". All told Glassell caught 10 broadbill at Cabo

Blanco, including fish of 610 and 687lb. Glassell never went more than three and half hours on a caught fish although he lost a Chilean broadbill after four and three-quarters.

A black marlin is harpooned off Cabo Blanco, it weighs in at 2250lb.

1954 Lou Marron's wife, Eugenie catches 772lb broadbill the new woman's record and still the woman's 80lb (37kg) line record.

1955 Kip Farrington is decorated by the Peruvian Government for promoting Peru's offshore big game fishing.

The Big Fish

1182lb Louis Marron 1953 Chile current 130lb record

937lb Arthur Hall 1953 Chile old 130lb record

860lb W.E.S. Tuker 1940 Chile old 130lb record

853lb S Kip Farrington 1941 Chile

849lb George Garey 1938 Chile

842lb George Garey 1936 Chile old 130lb record

837lb 8oz W.E.S. Tuker 1934 Chile old 130lb record

8??lbs George Garey 193? Chile (exact details unknown)

813lb 7oz Gerald Garrett 2003 New Zealand current 80lb record

781lb Mrs Marilyn Grant 1953 Chile disqualified

780lb Don Allison 1952 Chile

772lb Robert Brane 1952 Chile

772lb Eugenie Marron 1954 Chile current 80lb record

759lb Mrs Millie Allison 1952 Chile current 130lb record

758lb Alfred Glassell 1952 Chile

748lb Holt Jewell 1952 Chile

741lb Clarence Ellis 1941 Chile

732lb 12oz Murray Hansen 2001 New Zealand old 80lb record

732lb Jack Anderson 1952 Chile

705lb 8oz Alan Ralston 2004 New Zealand disqualified

Other Notable Broadbill Swordfish Captures on Rod and Line

696lb Mrs F Crowder 1952 Chile 180lb test line

687lb Alfred Glassell 1951 Peru

683lb Sr. Grazziani 1953 Chile

676lb 12oz T. Franich 2002 New Zealand current Junior Record

674lb Harlan Major 1934 Chile

672lb W.E.S. Tuker 1934 Chile

671lb 9oz H. White-Wickham 1928 New Zealand old 130lb record

665lb Louis Marron 1953 Chile

659lb Sara Farrington 1941 Chile 80lb test line

658lb Michael Lerner 1940 Chile

657lb F. Cameron 1989 Chile old 80lb test line record

651lb Clarence Ellis 1941 Chile

650lb 5oz H R Philips 1987 Chile old 80lb test line record

646lb Albert Little 1972 N.E. USA (unconfirmed)

643lb Tom Gregory 2001 New Zealand 80lb test line-disqualified

645lb 8oz Ian O'Brien 1998 New Zealand current 50lb record

640lb 4oz Martin Hirsch 2004 New Zealand 130lb test

638lb Michael Lerner 1940 Peru

631lb 6oz Laurie Stephens 2001 New Zealand 80lb test line

629lb 4oz John McClaren 2004 New Zealand 80lb test line

628lb Federico Weisner 1953 Chile

626lb Don Allison 1952 Chile

625lb Thelma Krieger 1953 Chile

622lb S. Kip Farrington 1953 Peru

619lb W.E.S. Tuker 1933 Chile

617lb S. Kip Farrington 1941 Chile

617lb S. Kip Farrington 1941 Chile

617lb Luis Verdigo 1953 Chile

615lb F.W. Utz 1938 Chile

612lb 12oz S. Sandford 1978 Florida old 80lb test line record

610lb Alfred Glassell 1953 Peru

608lb 8oz Martin Hirsch 2005 New Zealand

601lb Michael Lerner 1940 Nova Scotia old Atlantic record

562lb 8oz J. Johnson 1977 Florida old 80lb test line record

530lb W Margulies 1960 Montauk USA old 80lb test line record

533lb 8oz C McAdams 1988 Chile 50lb test line record

492lb 4oz Mrs D Cassullo 1959 Montauk USA 50lb test line record

Map labels

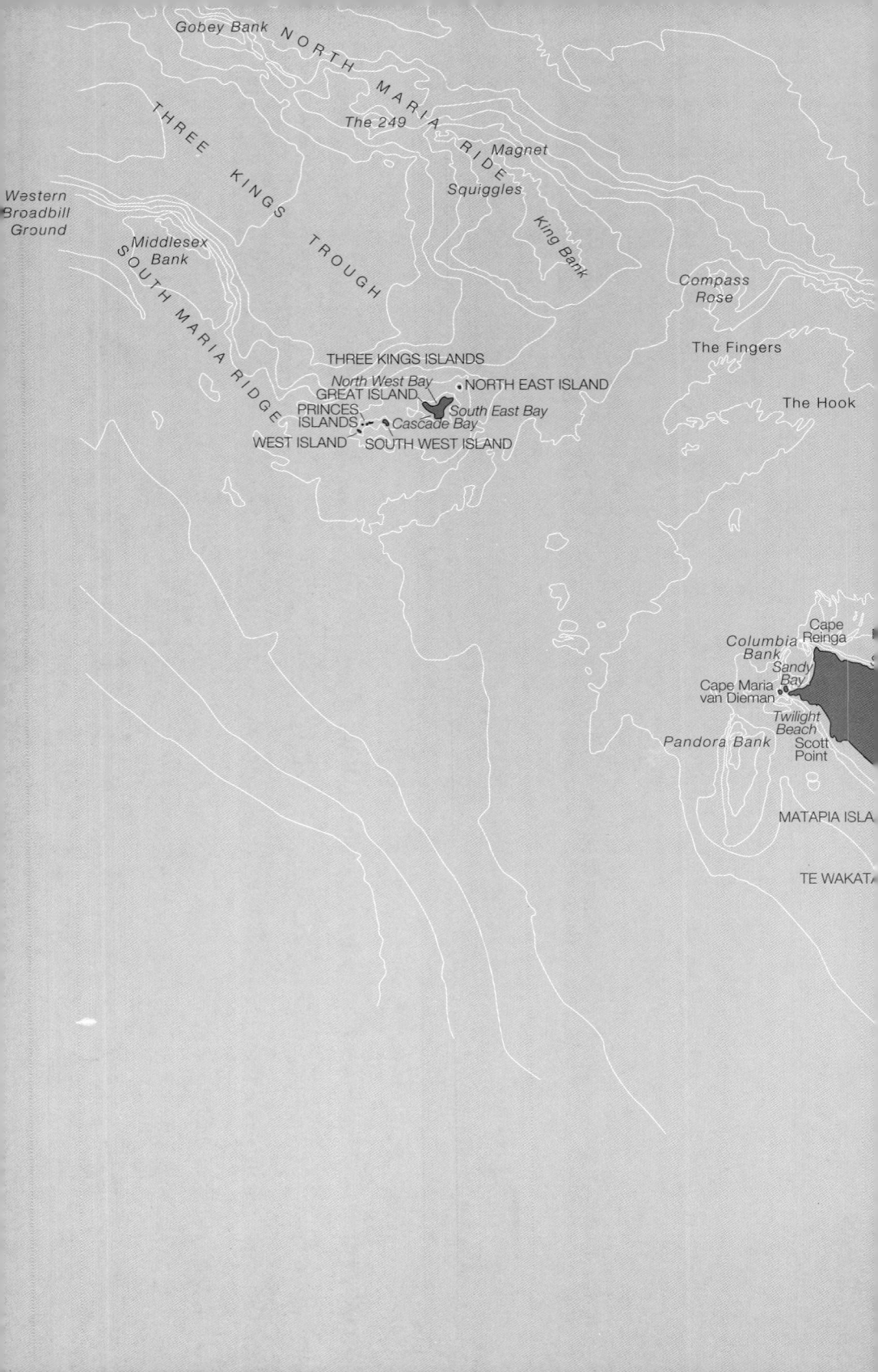

Gobey Bank
NORTH MARIA RIDGE
The 249
Magnet
Squiggles
Western Broadbill Ground
THREE KINGS TROUGH
Middlesex Bank
King Bank
Compass Rose
SOUTH MARIA RIDGE
The Fingers
THREE KINGS ISLANDS
North West Bay
GREAT ISLAND
NORTH EAST ISLAND
The Hook
PRINCES ISLANDS
South East Bay
Cascade Bay
WEST ISLAND
SOUTH WEST ISLAND
Columbia Bank
Cape Reinga
Sandy Bay
Cape Maria van Dieman
Twilight Beach
Scott Point
Pandora Bank
MATAPIA ISLA
TE WAKAT

Fingers

The Hook

Columbia Bank
Cape Reinga
PANANEHE ISLAND
Sandy Bay
Spirits Bay
Tom Bowling Bay
Surville Cliffs
North Cape
MURIMOTU ISLAND
Parengarenga Canyons

pe Maria
n Dieman
Twilight Beach
Scott Point
Ohao Point
PARENGARENGA HARBOUR

a Bank

MATAPIA ISLAND

GREAT EXHIBITION BAY

Garden Patch

505

TE WAKATAHAUA ISLAND
THE BLUFF

200m

RANGAUNU BAY
Mount Camel

MORUROA ISLANDS
Cape Karikari

Knuckle Point

100m

RANGAUNU HARBOUR

DOUBTLESS BAY
Berghans Point
Fair Way Reef
Wekarua

AHIPARA BAY

Whangaroa Seamount

60 Mile Ground

Cavalli Seamount

505
500m
400m
300m

Sea Mount

Clayworks

Ruahine Shoal

Nine Pin Trench

Wekarua STEPHENSON ISLAND
FLATHEAD ISLAND
Taheka Rock
WHANGAROA BAY
Donahues
CAVALLI ISLANDS
MOTOKAWAITI ISLAND
TAKOU BAY

Knight's Terrace

Main Rock

Queen's Buoy

NINEPIN
BAY OF ISLANDS
Onslow Rock
Cape Brett